Once A Marine

By Levi E. Hemrick

Foreword to the New Edition by
Charles Culbertson

Clarion Publishing
Staunton, Virginia

Table of Contents

Foreword to the New Edition of
Once A Marine

When I was a boy in the late 1950s, my mother and I would frequently cross Mitchell Bridge Road in Athens, Georgia, to visit our favorite neighbors, Levi and Elizabeth Hemrick. The Hemricks lived in an attractive brick home surrounded by shade trees and immaculately maintained gardens, and while my mother and Mrs. Hemrick chatted inside, Mr. Hemrick would take me outside for a tour of his prized flower beds. He would patiently tell me the names of the flowers, and then quiz me on them as we made a second go-around. I'm afraid I didn't do very well on the quizzes, but Mr. Hemrick never seemed to mind. The joy for him was sharing the beauty of his labors, even with a small, not-very-attentive boy.

In his late 60s when I first met him, Mr. Hemrick – to this day I can't refer to him as, simply, "Hemrick" – was a tall, large-boned man with broad, kind features and one of the warmest smiles I have ever seen. At first I didn't heed the ever-present hearing aid in his left ear (it was much like the one my own grandfather wore), or the deep white scars that scored his right arm, but as I got older and began to slough off the most inattentive part of childhood, I asked him about them. That's when I learned that the nice old man I had known for years was a combat veteran of World War I. More than that, he had been a United States Marine, which in my young eyes set him far apart from the garden variety military veteran.

Now, instead of tours of the Hemrick flower beds, I was treated to afternoons of war stories over a checkerboard in Mr. Hemrick's thoroughly masculine study. Filled with books, illustrations, cigar smoke and rich, dark wood, the room was anchored by an antique roll-top desk that held – in addition to a hodgepodge of papers – a handful of fading black-and-white photographs. These photographs were of soldiers in a variety of combat poses. Some appeared to fight hand-to-hand; others lay prone in the dirt firing rifles. Yet others worked the mechanisms of large guns. As I thumbed through these photographs, Mr. Hemrick told me they had been taken during the filming of a movie of which he had been a part. The film, a World War I propaganda/fund-raiser under the title *What Price Glory?*, had

1

used members of Mr. Hemrick's Marine Corps unit as its cast. He said if I could ever find the film, which he himself hadn't seen since 1917, I could pick him out in several key scenes.

In about 1967 – we had long since moved to Staunton, Virginia – we returned to Mitchell Bridge Road for a visit with the Hemricks. Nothing had changed. The home was still neat as a pin, the gardens still immaculate, the study still everything a man could want. The grand old gentleman hadn't changed, either, except that now, instead of wanting me to look at his flowers or play checkers while listening to war stories, he wanted me to look at a manuscript. He thrust into my hands a sheaf of typewritten pages that he said contained his World War I memoir, and then went outside to inspect his gardens while I sat in the study and read his book. Well, it *was* a book, I was a fidgety fifteen-year-old, and there wasn't much perusal I could do in the half hour or so available to me. But I did give it a go. I read as much of it as I could, skipping here and there to get the essence of the work, and then, when Mr. Hemrick came back inside, told him what a great job I thought he'd done.

The following year, 1968, he had the book published and gave an inscribed copy of *Once A Marine* to my mother. By this time I was toying with the idea of joining the Marine Corps after high school, and I'm sure that Mr. Hemrick's memoir played a part in my decision to do so.

Many years would pass before I again picked up *Once A Marine*. This time, with the eyes and experience of a man in his early 60s, I read and re-read the book, devouring my old friend's descriptions of his time in the Great War. Of particular interest to me was his chronicle of the making of *What Price Glory*? A little research revealed that the film – which may now be lost, or reposing in the oblivion of a vault somewhere – was most likely a production of the U.S. Committee on Public Information.

"In one part," wrote Mr. Hemrick, "I was in a machine gun squad, in which I and another Marine were pulling a two-wheel, rubber-tired cart carrying a Lewis machine gun (which was never used by us in France). In another scene, I was fighting with a rifle with bayonet attached, charging the Germans down an incline. In this scene I was to be killed. When I reached a proper place to die,

I pitched myself forward as one would when felled to the ground while running. As I fell I rammed my bayonet into the ground and let go. This left the rifle sticking in the ground with the butt standing quivering in the air, leaving a marker that stood there throughout the scene."

If anyone ever finds the film, and if it's in good enough condition to be watched, look for the guy ramming his rifle, bayonet first, into the ground. That's Levi Hemrick.

In returning this book to print, I have changed very little of the original text. Occasionally there was a typographical error, or a misspelling, and I have corrected those. Also, Mr. Hemrick was not overly fond of commas and let many of his sentences go farther than perhaps was prudent, so I have added one or two for the sake of readability. Except for those minor edits, the narrative is precisely as Mr. Hemrick wrote it.

The re-publication of *Once A Marine* is, for me, a labor of love because I knew and loved its author. I like to think he'd be happy that the small boy who wandered through his garden with him and played checkers with him grew up to be a writer, and helped preserve his memoir.

For you, the reader, I hope this re-publication opens afresh an avenue of knowledge about the First World War that, for many years, has been closed to public view, and that you come to appreciate Levi Hemrick and his contribution to the winning of the Great War as much as I do.

Charles Culbertson
Staunton, Virginia
December 2013

Introduction

This is an ex-Devil Dog Marine's answer to a Double Dog Dare to tell a story that ought to be told of a common man, a private in the ranks.

War is an ugly, deadly plague. It is something to run from, avoid contact with, and isolate from, but – as long as the danger of war exists – to be prepared for, and to fight like hell, if it should come to our country.

War is brewed in the devil's pot, attended by his imps, some of whom wear saintly robes. But, rest assured, no real saints attend that pot.

This is not a typical war story, neither is it history. But it is full of facts and incidents not usually found in history books. Some of it you will enjoy, other parts may make you angry. But remember, you too may profit by just a wee bit of needling.

Prologue

I decided to take as my hobby the writing of my World War I experience. But in spite of my resolved purpose to tell a simple story of a simple man and write the story of a common soldier in a very significant war, I quickly discovered that the private soldier was not very simple; on the contrary, he was a compounded mixture of two persons; an inner man and the outer man. Though the inner man is often completely ignored and treated as if it did not exist, it is by far the most important part of a fighting soldier. And of all men, in all professions, the soldier is the least able to survive without the aid of his philosophy. So I cannot portray a common man in the fighting garb of his country without talking about the inner man and a soldier's philosophy.

A soldier's philosophy is as much a part of him and is as important to a foot soldier as are his feet and legs. I learned these facts the hard way, by personal experience, and from a teacher that does not make mistakes. I am against the idea that philosophy is only for Ph.D.s arrived at through seminars and endowed research. In common folk's language, a man's philosophy is his plotted course and acts as his guideline to keep him on a straight path as he wanders along the unmarked roadways of life.

One purpose of this manuscript is to record for posterity my own moral, religious, political and soldier philosophy. Now, don't close these pages and run; it really is a philosophy of common sense, often possessed by men who have never learned their A.B.C.

The story is about me, my wartime experience, my answer to the question, "Daddy, what did you do in the War?" But it goes beyond that and attempts to give a life-like picture of the common soldier and not just one person's daddy.

The story part is told in episodes that actually happened to me in World War I. It covers the days spent in a Marine boot camp, on the battlefields of France, as well as the incidents along the way; and ends in a hospital bed and a short time in "Paree."

While sex, rascality, brutality, drunkenness, heroism and cowardice are a part of every war, in our war these things played but a minor role in the lives of the men with whom I associated during

7

my two years' service in the Marine Corps. I shall give them the space they deserve.

Since this is my story, about me, it is proper to use the pronoun 'I,' and write the story from my personal point of view. The little soldier has his big moments and adventures which don't always coincide with those of the major battles and events. Though hard fought battles get big publicity, the easy ones are the common soldier's delight. His personal big moments are usually ignored by the press and historians. A private saving another private's life in close combat is about as common as dog biting man, and rates about the same publicity.

The generals, heroes, poets, historians, politicians, and professional writers have had their day and collected their reward. Now the chow-hounds, stretcher-bearers, and privates in the ranks should have theirs. That is another reason for this story.

A hot slug propelled from the angry mouth of a German field gun wrote the finish to my Marine Corps career. I am now a retired breadwinner turned writer, a hobby-horse rider who hopes to forget about present day worries long enough each day to ride the old war-time trail that led to and through World War I.

Every incident and episode recorded is my personal experience with real people, and is as accurate in detail as my memory will permit. In those cases where it is expedient or advisable to do so I have substituted fictitious names for real names to avoid possible embarrassment to the people involved. Then, too, this is about common soldiers and only for special reasons do I rope in personalities.

People are not born patriots and it is foolish to pretend that they are. Neither are all people born with an equal amount of guts; some seem to have little brain-power or guts to speak of. Whatever the amount each has, all enlisted men or draftees into military service must have some.

In schools, on tough jobs, and in boot camp, it is known what proper exercise can mean to guts and the will to do – the same thing that fertilizer means to plants. It stimulates their growth.

In the following chapters as you accompany me through my basic military training you will see guts stimulated and made to grow. You will also see how self-discipline was boosted by being forced to do disagreeable tasks. The drop outs have formed the habit of resisting authority. We were forced into the habit of submitting to authority. That habit becomes such a force that we would obey orders that meant almost certain death. DISCIPLINE is the key which unlocks the power and force that enables the will to do and the guts to carry on when the going is tough and the body is weakest.

Chapter 1

The war of 1914, which we entered in 1917, solved none of the old problems. Unlike World War II, there was no Adolf Hitler to take all the blame for it. Our chief objective in World War I was "Get Rid of the Kaiser," which as it turned out made it possible for the rise of Hitler to power and the spread of communism, which proved to be the worst thing that could have happened to Europe and the rest of the world.

It was a sobering shock when Congress declared war on Germany on April 6, 1917. Most of us knew that our government had taken no real steps to make ready for war. We were led to believe President Wilson's idea was to furnish food and supplies to the Allies and perhaps a token force of soldiers. We felt strongly that the Allies had all the soldiers needed to defeat Germany. The United States had no General of the Army, but Colonel John Pershing was quickly promoted to that rank. He with a few army regulars – soldiers with practically no arms – landed in Europe just ten days after I begged a ride on a milk truck to Atlanta and enlisted in the armed forces.

Men in the first group to land in France later fought with the First Army Division which saw its first real fighting approximately eleven months later, that is about four days before my division, the Second Army Division, engaged in serious fighting with the enemy.

Prior to my enlistment, I held the position of principal in a three teacher rural school in Panthersville, DeKalb County, Georgia. This small hamlet was about four miles south of Decatur and about ten miles south by east of Atlanta. Two-thirds of the people in the community were small farm families. Most of these families operated small dairy and truck farms and, aside from growing the greater part of their own foodstuff, produced a small amount of cotton. None were rich but all lived well and within their means. It was a law-abiding community. All the young people, as their elders, behaved because that was considered the proper thing to do.

From the beginning of the European war, a few people were anxious for this country to enter it but were held in check by the peace sentiment of church groups. But when war was declared, the war mongers went all out to rouse the American public.

School teachers then, as now, were in short supply, and about as indispensable as any special group one could name. Being a member of that group I had not given a thought to becoming a soldier prior to the draft act of 1917. With the passage of this act, however, I was forced to come to grip with some deeply personal questions.

If Uncle Sam was going to need thousands of men to help win the war, should one of them be me? Should I ask for exemption on the basis of my job? After careful consideration, my answer to the first question was yes; to the second was no. My decision was made. I set about clearing up my obligations to the school and taking care of other more personal matters. Then, conscience free, I hitched that fateful ride to Atlanta on a milk truck and presented myself to a Marine sergeant at the recruiting station and enlisted in the Marines for the duration of the war.

I would be less than truthful if I did not admit that patriotism was not the only motivation for my enlistment in the Marines. I suppose every young fellow has dreams of visiting far off places. In my younger days, it was true that if given the chance of an expense paid visit to any city of his choice, any young man would have unhesitatingly chosen Paris, France. So, going to war also meant going to France, going to Paris, the city of my dreams. As proof that a lot of other fellows felt that way, I will recall to your memory that popular World War One song, *How You Gonna Keep 'Em Down On the Farm After They've Seen Paree?*

While I might have been naive, I was not wholly ignorant of what becoming a military man would mean to me. When I boarded that train in Atlanta and headed for boot camp at Parris Island, I was fully aware that I was traveling on a one-way ticket. I knew when I shed my civilian clothes for a soldier's uniform other less tangible things would be shed too. Body posture, speech, taste, attitude, mannerisms, outlook on life, all were to undergo change. Some changes would be profitable and would show up in many ways the rest of my life.

But what of the other side of the ledger, the loss column? What would war do to my soul? What would war do to my mind, my spirit? Could I become a mean fighter without becoming a mean man? Could I kill without becoming a killer? These and other disturbing questions nagged my mind as the train clacked along the rails widening the gap between Panthersville and Parris Island.

Changing from civilian to military life can be a shocking experience. The rich and the poor, the educated and the illiterates, the cultured and the rough necks, the religious and the infidels, the farmers and city slickers, all are forced into intimate association. The cultured grow less refined, the slovenly become tidy. The educated add slang to their vocabularies, the unschooled improve. The over-weights grow slim, the slender ones fill out. The stoop-shouldered straighten up, and the stiff backs loosen up. Pot bellies and big behinds are pulled in and caved chests are thrown out. There is a leveling off process all along the line. Thus it is that extremes are eliminated making a close similarity of the men who wear service uniforms. Male ruggedness and physical fitness is the goal of every boot camp, all men envy it and the fairest women fall for it.

In the truest sense, I was a prisoner of war for I had   joined for the duration. To be sure I was a volunteer prisoner of war, but like thousands of others I looked forward to release and freedom. Emotionally we were waiting for peace like children waiting for Christmas to come. There were periods when time passed very slowly, but we knew that our service time could be shortened or lengthened by ourselves. We knew our release had a price tag on it, winning a fighting victory over the Germans. So we naturally had a deep desire to get to the front, beat the Boche, and go home.

Even so, war has its moments of triumphs, excitement and fun. I had my full share of each. What I will endeavor to do in the following chapters is to balance the ledger by showing the bitter and sweet; love and hate ; the joy and sorrow ; triumphs and defeats, as they come and as they apply to me, our country and the individual soldier's body and soul. Too many people try to ignore the fact that a human being has two selves, his physical body and his spiritual one. We don't bury a man, only his body is placed beneath the cold, cold earth. War's mental agonies leave a deeper scar than the bodily hurts that are administered to its victims.

Chapter 2

The first leg of the journey was over when the train ground to a steaming, hissing stop at the Beauford, South Carolina station. As I reached for my suitcase overhead, I glanced out the window and saw three Marines standing smartly on the station platform. The tallest one, wearing a sergeant's chevrons, called out, "All out for Parris Island."

With about thirty or forty other men with suitcases in hand, I got off the train. As each of us stepped down we were told to answer our names and form a line facing the sergeant. After roll call we were marched down to the docks where we boarded a motor launch and headed for Parris Island.

The short trip to boot camp was uneventful but our excitement mounted as we neared the wharf. As the launch nosed in to its landing, we were greeted by a howling mob of recent recruits gathered at the top of the gangway to welcome us to the Marine Corps. You can bet that welcoming committee bore no resemblance to dignified, gold braided post officials welcoming a Congressional Committee! We didn't rate that high but, by gosh, we deserved more than we received! We were disgusted, a little scared, but mostly disheartened by that noisy, ragged-pants bunch. We had come from as far away as Wisconsin's dairy farms and the panhandle of Texas and this, this was the welcome we got! What our welcoming committee lacked in quality was made up by numbers. What it lacked in dignity was replaced by enthusiastic vulgarity. Instead of a brass band our tender civilian ears were assaulted by a horrible chanted rhyme, not the least delicate of our greetings: "You'll never get rich, you son of a bitch, you're in the army now!"

From the head of the gangway to the street (a good two hundred feet) this raucous, jeering mob formed two lines with a narrow path between. We had no choice but to march single file up that narrow path between those wild juveniles playing Indians. In their eyes we were legitimate prey – candidates for their version of initiation into Parris Island's Brotherhood of Marines.

Then the initiation began. Armed with tightly rolled newspapers, rubber hoses, ropes or other handy tools of torture, they lambasted us on all sides with well aimed blows as we hustled through. The fun was all theirs. We were too busy hanging onto our hats and dodging their   flails to enjoy it. As we ducked and stumbled along no blood was drawn; we suffered only slight bruises to our bodies – but the damage to our civilian pride and dignity was too terrible to describe. Even so, I think we could have endured it all with chins up if those wild bucks hadn't chanted in loud unison during it all that awful ditty: "You'll never get rich, you son of a bitch, you're in the army now!" That was the crowning insult and we slunk along behind the grinning sergeant like a pack of whipped curs.

Our group, with a few other of the day's recruits, was assigned to a tent large enough to shelter forty or fifty men. Still stinging from the initiation, we bunked down and were about settled for a much needed rest when an old timer Marine staggered in. His blouse sleeve was almost completely covered with hache marks. He was really soused or putting on the most realistic drunk act I have ever seen.

Sticking in the old fellow's service belt was the longest barreled, whopping big pistol I had ever seen. He pulled out that enormous hand gun, eyed us blearily, and carelessly pointed it at first one and then the other of us. Then, satisfied that he had our attention – and, believe me, he had it! – he reeled over to a table, sat down and faced us, pistol still in his hands. Suddenly, he banged on the table with the butt of the pistol and began to harangue us on the virtue and history of the Marine Corps, boasting of his own exploits and acts of heroism. We couldn't tell for sure whether he was actually drunk, acting out a wild-west type barroom scene, or just showing his true nature under the influence of alcohol. But whatever his reasons were for that display, I didn't enjoy it.

In fact, I was shocked, deeply shocked. This was a far cry from what I expected. Was this drunken slouch the real Marine? Was the poster in Atlanta and the recruiting officer's talk just window dressing to lure fellows like me into the Corps? Was this just another phase of our initiation to boot camp? These and other painful thoughts plagued me as the old fellow abruptly ended his thick-tongued lecture and lurched out of the tent. Our eyes slid past each other, none wishing to voice opinion or betray inmost thoughts. Finally, I dropped off into fitful sleep distraught in mind but too bone-tired to thresh this matter over any longer. I was almost convinced that the old Marine was just another soldier doing his part to initiate us.

Dawn, on the first and most important day on our prison island, found me awake. This was the day. This day we would know whether we were good enough to be accepted into that exclusive, most selective organization, the United States Marine Corps. A little of my eagerness returned, but, remembering yesterday, it was also tinged with apprehension. It was a bright, warm morning. Young roosters were greeting the sun and rousing the laying madams so they could start scratching for their quota of worms before getting down to the real business of the day. Bugles began to blare and corporals began banging on the tent walls yelling, "Hit the deck!"

This "treat them rough and they'll soon be tough" manner of awakening the troops was but the first of many rude awakenings for us. We piled out of our bunks rubbing sleep-swollen eyes and flinching against the sudden pain of yesterday's bruises. Had we but known this was just the first of many pain-wracked mornings perhaps our avid desire to become first-rate Marines would not have been so intense. We were to look back on this morning and realize our discomfort was trivial compared to what we later endured.

We dressed hurriedly, while a gravel-voiced corporal barked at us, and were herded to the mess tent where we were fed a breakfast of foul-smelling eggs, spuds boiled in their jackets, fried fat back and black coffee. Or should I use the language of the day and say that we were served: "hen fruit, spuds, punk, piss and sow belly"? After the meal, we were herded to the public water hydrant where we washed and shaved. From there, we marched back to the tent and made up our bunks, the area in and outside the tent picking up cigarette butts, paper and other litter we had strewn the night before.

So far, we had been under the corporal's direction entirely. We could not leave the tent area without his permission. After our clean-up detail was completed, he told us to remain in the tent until we received orders to report to the examining board.

For awhile we sat around, mostly silent, waiting for what was to come. Then there was a slight shifting at the front of the tent and a whispered, "This is it!" passed rapidly from bunk to bunk.

The tent flap swung aside and two neatly khaki clad men entered the tent, a sergeant and his aide. The sergeant's loud commanding, "ATTENTION!" brought each of us quickly to our feet. This was our first real military order and, rookies that we were, we recognized the real authority of that command. There were a few in the group who had previous military training. Their quick reaction to that order led us to give a ragged imitation which, at this late date, still makes me smile.

"You have been instructed to follow the corporal-in-charge's orders and not to leave the tent without his permission," the sergeant began. "Beginning now, you are under my direct orders. You will do what I tell you now. Each time I dismiss you, you will return to this tent and wait here for further orders from me. Now, you have fifteen minutes to smoke, get a drink of water, or go to the latrine. Later, you can't do any of these. Remember, FIFTEEN minutes! Dismissed."

When the fifteen minutes were up we certainly were not prepared for the sergeant's next order.

"Strip to the skin," he commanded. We looked at each other with puzzled eye. "Yes!" he barked, "to the skins, every mother's son of you! Get moving, get moving. We're going to take a little trip. You're to carry nothing but your naked barefoot selves. Come on, come on, get going!"

That motley group of modest, timid, skinny, fat, knock-kneed, bow-legged, hairy, hairless men began reluctantly to disrobe. An uglier conglomeration of the species has never been equaled! Ordered to form a single line as our names were called and to keep that order until we received our physical examinations and shots, the sergeant bawled, "Follow me!"

Meekly, in our stark nakedness, we fell in line and followed the sergeant for a distance of four or five blocks before we were halted in front of a barrack-like building to wait for the arrival of the doctors. Most of us were embarrassed and self-conscious as we stood there fumbling around and casting sheepish glances at our equally uncomfortable companions. Only those with broad chest, hard muscles, and obvious physical development seemed to enjoy the situation or to do any strutting. The rest of us just waited numbly until the door opened and the long line of men passed over the threshold to escape into the comparatively private interior and out of the glare of broad daylight.

Slowly the line snaked into the building to be met by a battery of physicians. Each of us received a thorough going over. Those sharp-eyed doctors missed nothing; well, hardly anything. For years there had been a swollen knot on the right side of my shank. I was able to conceal it somehow and passed the grade.

Heart, lungs ears, eyes, throats, scars, tattoo marks, birthmarks, everything was checked. We were punched, thumped and pummeled. One poor devil who knew that his eyesight was poor memorized the row of letters, used to test our sight, as he waited his turn. But the tricky doctor had changed the order of the letters before testing this man's eyes and the poor fellow completely failed the eye test.

We passed on down the line to be attacked by hard-boiled enlisted Marines who swabbed us with alcohol-soaked cotton, crisscrossed our arms with skin breakers, and stabbed us with virus-loaded needles. My blood stream showed its displeasure by later giving me a fevered brow, hateful headache and throbbing aches all over my body. Passing the examination and being accepted in the Marine Corps should have made me happy but my physical miseries were just too great to leave room for much joy.

In our follow-the-leader fashion, we tramped back to the tent, dressed, and in the same manner marched to our midday meal of Irish stew, prunes, bread and coffee. Then we returned to the tent for a few moments' rest. I thought I had had enough for that day, but was I ever so mistaken!

There were not enough tents for the war-time Marine Corps; new barracks were needed. So we were herded back into line, still dressed in our civilian clothes, and marched into a newly surveyed section of the island where new barracks were to be erected.

When we reached the site, we found piles and piles of freshly sawed green or half-green lumber, still oozing globs of sticky resin. Our protesting muscles were put to work moving that heavy, gummy, stuffy lumber from "where it was to where it ain't" without further ado. Without warning, we soda jerkers, sales clerks, office boys and flabby muscled ex-school teachers were turned into a bunch of pack-

18

mules! Sure, we had passed our physical examinations but this was the real test.

Had we the spirit, the stamina and guts of which Marines are created? Could we make it – that do or die required of Marines? Yea! But darn it, this had begun to look like we would do and die! Oh, we stood the test, we didn't walk off the job, we weren't drop-outs, fall-outs or quitters. That is, only one guys guts failed him. Maybe his will to do wasn't sufficiently backed by pride, self-respect and practiced self-discipline. Anyway, he walked away from that tough job as any undisciplined weakling is prone to do when his lessons get hard in school, his muscles get tired at the work bench, or his team's captain wants him to practice more.

Our drop-out had the physique for the job but the spirit was lacking. As for intelligence, it seems he had enough to carry out his plan to get what he wanted. But let me give you the story as it was told to me at the time. From the time he quit the job he seemed like a harmless idiot. His face was expressionless; he spoke to no one; he ignored all remarks addressed to him. His only activity seemed to be a continual search for something. He plodded around the area ceaselessly, hunting, hunting, hunting. Every time he spied a piece of paper, large or small, he grabbed it, feverishly examined it and was heard by some one to mutter, "This ain't it." Then, as the story continues, he was seen coming out of headquarters one day with some papers in his hand. He sat down, stared at them intently, then leaped to his feet muttering excitedly, "This is it !" These papers were his medical discharge from the Marine Corps.

I had been on the Island only a few days when I made a blunder on a detail. Politely, in my ingrained civilian way, I began an apology with, "I beg your pardon." I was cut short with "Pardon, hell! We don't grant pardons in this outfit." This began my indoctrination in the Marine Corps' successful method of issuing a challenge to an individual and daring him to prove himself a man of strength. Sympathy has no place in a Marine sergeant's vocabulary. The Corps makes men out of boys and sissies.

The seeming cruelties imposed on us recruits, the suffering we endured, the indignities inflicted on our aching bodies and the apparent raw deal handed us at the lumber pile were necessary. Yes, all of it: the insults to our civilian pride, the jar to our self-conceit and the endurance tests we had to pass, marked the ending of civilian weakness such as that Caesar deplored. There were many more lessons to follow, one isn't enough. First you are taught to know the lesson, then you follow up with practice in order to establish mental habits and adjustments that make such things a part of one's emotional self. There had to be more, to develop a hard body to fit the image of an American Marine. A change had to occur within the man as well as on the outside.

A soldier's body minus a soldier's mind and spirit would be a strutting zombie, a parading statue of paper strength. He would be useless as a fighter in the hour of greatest need. At Parris Island we gained not only the body but the mind and will and the tearing, grinding agonies we endured were the crucible.

Permit me to say to our church people: A soldier that does not carry the spirit of his country in his bosom and a spirit of submission to the will of his country, is comparable to a soldier of Christ that does not carry the spirit of Christ in his heart and is not submissive to the will of God.

Chapter 3

Due to shortage and delay in the arrival of service clothes, we were forced to wear our civilian garb for several days and our civilian shoes for many days. They were wholly unsuited for the work that we had to do, and especially so, because of the hot dusty weather that accompanied the June temperatures of that year.

Our tight-fitting, thin-sole civilian shoes were one continuous torment. Our corns and bunions became fiery red and so sensitive to the tight grip of our shoes that we could hardly stand it. Then there followed big water blisters from a dime to a half-dollar in size. Though my shoes stretched little, if any, my feet under the trod, trod, cadence, sound off of stamp, stamp, and orders to put 'em down hard, became bigger as the days went by. And when night came the task of pulling a number seven shoe from a number ten foot was a living nightmare. But there was no pity shown or sympathy expressed for us. No let-up in the amount of drill or work toil required for us. "We were in the army now." A war was in progress in Europe, our manhood was on trial. "Were we jelly fish? Had we the guts to be Marines?" It was do or die, so we did.

In time a supply of shoes came through for us. One peep at the lot and I nearly passed out. They were old-time, double-soled brogans, the kind slaves used to wear. Their leather was as stiff as cardboards and as tough as plywood. To put my tender feet along with my bunions, corns and blisters inside of them was more than I thought I could stand. But what else could one do? I wasn't in the mood to die, not yet. So instead of asking for number sevens like I was wearing at the time of my enlistment, I ask for number elevens and that was what I got. Next I put on three pairs of thick, white cotton socks.

Well, brother, those shoes were plenty heavy and my feet got awfully hot and tired but in no time the suffering was eased and I was taught another lesson. "Even misery has its rewards," as was proved by my demonstration through this experience. As the soreness left, the blisters disappeared, the corns and bunions vanished and my feet became sound and tough, and though that was better than forty-eight years ago, I have never had foot blister, corn or bunion since. I never got back to number seven shoe or real thin socks again. My number settled down to a permanent number ten. This shoe with soft, thick socks, even in summer time, became my standard footwear and I look back with pleasure to the year 1917 when I received my first important lesson in Brogueology.

The enormous increase in the men brought to the island made the toilet facilities wholly inadequate. As a substitute to our old fashioned outhouse or privy, we had a six-foot plank walk-way flanked by flimsy hand railings that led out some hundred or more feet over the Atlantic Ocean. During low tide the long stilts upon which this platform was built put one twenty feet up in the air and at high tide, the wind and spray just didn't add one thing to one's comfort. The two or three times a day one had to make a trip out over the water and stand or squat exposed to the wind and spray, to say nothing of a downward look at those fast moving waves, was a nerve wrecking experience of never-to-be-forgotten discomfort and dread, but this, too, was an important part of our training. For a time would come of exposure to enemy fire, especially an unprincipled German sniper watching our out-of-trench latrine for a shot and victim. Such has been my experience and that of hundreds of others of the Marines who walked that plank way out over the waters of the Atlantic Ocean. All fighting men will go along with me in that, "It ain't fair to attack a man with his britches down."

Of course, these make-shift arrangements were hazardous and wholly unsatisfactory and it fell to our lot to help remedy it. It takes a big hole, in fact several holes, to hold a disposal plant designed to accommodate the sewage of several thousand men. It was a rush job, and picks, shovels and wheel-barrows were limited in number and, too, there is only a limited amount of working room in even a large hold, which made it advisable to work at the job around the clock in shifts of working crews. With the aid of acetylene lights, it was possible to do a scheduled amount of work at night. The different training companies performed and labored in four shifts around the clock. This was hard work, tiresome and hot; a real muscle making and body toughening task. My company drew a night shift and thus escaped the most unbearable heat of working in the hole in the hottest part of the day. In due time the sewage disposal plant was finished, modern toilets, showers and laundry tables and decent drinking was in abundance. But let's drop back to an earlier period and touch on a few other of the discomforts suffered on the island.

At one time, our source of drinking water was a shallow hand pump from a coastal well. The water tasted awful, but walking soldiers should not drink much water, a lesson the sooner he learned the less painful would be the long hikes and periods when there was none available. The Marine trainers were wise guys. A fellow would take a drink of this muddy-looking, foul-smelling, obnoxious stuff, only when he found it necessary to do so. The net result was a self-restricted denial and self-restraining drinking habits. We managed during those dry, hot June and July days to get by most of the time with three cups of coffee per day served with our meals. It appears, at times, that unplanned hardships are better and do the teaching job more efficiently than those planned. It is certainly better for one to refuse water of his own choice because of its taste than to have it denied him because some person in command says he cannot have it.

While the engineers, carpenters, plumbers and their aides were hammering away building bunk barracks, bath and wash houses and putting in sewage and water lines for the daily arriving new recruits, we early recruits were living in a most primitive style, squatted down on an island of sand. The old military facilities including the post office, church and swimming pool were out of bounds for us. In fact the brig only would accept us as welcome guest. Sunday was just another day, a work day, with barges to unload, holes to be dug and other emergency tasks to be performed. We, however, soon caught on to the church "racket." Nothing like that is advertised, except by word of mouth. A sneaked word gotten to the Catholic priest would get one a church service permit and pass into the restricted area of the post and out of work during the Sunday morning hours. This good Catholic priest was never known to discriminate against any Protestant or Jew. All religious faiths were accepted and given a service any and all could accept including the Jews. After the all-faiths' service, the Catholic service was performed for the benefit of those who remained for it.

During the hot dry summer, the mixture of sweat, sand and dust made it feasible if not necessary that we bathe and wash our

23

clothes every day. Our small tents were so small and crowded that there was not room in it for a bucket of water. All of our shaving, bathing and laundry work was done on the outside in the open space between ours and the neighbor's tent. A shortage of underwear in many cases, one change per man, added to our laundry problem. In general, it was customary at the end of the afternoon drill period for the whole company to fill their buckets with water, remove and wash their clothes and then proceed to bathe their bodies, all in the open. And all having their freshly washed garments inspected as they finished their task. On the island every recruit had to wash his own clothes. Later at Quantico, some of the fellows who wanted to make a little extra money would take-in washing from those who did not want to do their own laundry work.

Part of the time this clothes washing was done down on the ocean beach where there were great piles of oyster shells. When we were ready to go back to our tents, we would fill our buckets with shells and carry them back and dump them in our company's street before our tent.

Fire drills were quite common and everyone was expected when the bugle call sounded a fire call to go to the point of concentration. These drills were not practiced at an hour when most of the men were scheduled to be taking a bath. However, there are always a number of people who for one reason or another are caught napping. So, it was not unusual to see one of these armed with his fire bucket and dressed only in his shoes and a broad brimmed hat go galloping down the main camp street in answer to a bugle's fire call. Whatever the reason, the male species presents a comical reaction when he goes galloping down a street wearing only shoes and a broad brimmed hat. There are always some men ready to whoop it up and to add to a diversion from normal when the unusual comes along. A nude man carrying a bucket, especially wearing a tall or broad brimmed hat seem to furnish the incongruity that makes the action ridiculous and funny.

The island should not be visualized as an island of total gloom and grim torture, but as a place where sissies and boys are made into men. A place where people on leaving have few regrets, but admire, respect and appreciate the products of its labor. The island is a workshop and not a playground for pleasure-seeking playboys. A tough school turns out tough graduates. We live in a competitive, cruel world and to stand a hand with other tough people we in America must also be tough, and the surest way to make a young fellow tough is to treat him rough.

Our section was out of bounds to all visitors and I doubt if any ever set eyes on us. For ten weeks, a few days more or less, we were justified in calling it a prison camp. Our section was bound on three sides by the Atlantic Ocean and sea marshes, and the other side had its military police and it took a pass to get by them.

In close-order drills, everyone has his place and for any one to get out of place, in time, step or movement, he is stepped on or given a jolt by the fellow whose place he is trying to share. After a time, such movements become a fixed habit and one may march along hardly conscious of what he is doing or of what is taking place and yet perform in a perfect proper order movements with the others. It takes time and a lot of practice for a beginner to reach a point when he depends on fixed habits to keep him in step and proper timing and in his exact position where the pattern of the drill dictates. All of us rookies just hadn't had enough time and practice to have reached this point in the training where fixed habits took over and his thoughts are left to wander around on other matters.

We had just been issued our brand new Springfield rifles and were for the first time going to be put through all of the usual close-order drills carrying a rifle. Honestly, I don't know how it happened, there were seconds when I didn't know anything. It certainly could have been my thoughts had wandered off and I was caught napping, or it could have been the other fellow that was at fault.

All I know for certain about the episode is that some fellow's rifle and my head tried to occupy the same space and I was practically knocked to my knees and went staggering out of line with a head jar that for seconds dulled my ability to adjust myself to the situation. In the seconds it took for me to regain control of myself and while in the act of straightening up, the drill corporal rushed up and hit me in the back of my head with his fist, thus adding insult to injury. While the blow on the side of my head was close to a knock-out and had brought tears to my eyes, it was part of a rough game we were engaged in. The fist blow was a deliberate personal assault and recognized as such. My natural reaction was to whirl around and at the same time bring my rifle in position to smash in the corporal's face. Our eyes locked for seconds; the corporal dropped his hands, turned and walked to his place and I walked back to my place in the line.

In the short period of a few weeks, we noticed great changes on the island. The old plank walk out to the "head" whose raw sewage dropped into the Atlantic Ocean was gone, and a modern water toilet had taken its place. The small tents had been folded and packed away in safe keeping for some future date when they again will be the only shelter available for some Marines. The tent cots with their canvas cloth mattresses are now stacked in a storage room somewhere. In their place are nice clean barracks furnished with a double row of regular iron bunks, each with cotton mattress, and two clean blankets. Between the two long rows of bunks is a wide alley that provides space for each occupant at the foot of his bunk to keep a storage locker or sea bag for his clothes and other private possessions, and still leave room for an officer to come by on an inspection tour. Nothing fancy, to the eyes of a city dude and yet a whale of an improvement over a pup tent. A real luxury in comparison to a camp cot, dirt floor, stooping head room and a squeezed-in-body posture in the limited space of a pup tent's confines.

We now had an abundance of clothes, full of wrinkles and not fitting very well. Washed, rather than the more dignified term laundered, by us. Worn without having been ironed or pressed. The fat boys had worked and sweated off big chunks of their weight, leaving their uniforms baggy. The lean ones broadened out and developed sizable muscles which left their garments too tight. We had no dress-up company clothes. It happened that none of us had ever asked for a liberty pass. The reason was we had nothing to wear that we would have been caught in outside our camp.

Our brogans had worsened in looks, they refused to take a shine, but in time adjusted themselves to our feet. Perhaps it was the other way around, our feet had become adjusted to them. The day by day wearing of them became a fixed habit, so much so that we no longer took notice of them. Their thickness gave them a protection that made them ideal for our purpose. We, of course, had no delusions about their looks and cared less, for we knew that we weren't going anywhere until Uncle Sam saw fit to give us a pair of dress shoes.

The sun, the heat, the tramp, tramp, and double-time drill from daybreak to late in the afternoon and then to our daily laundry tour for six days per week and Sunday work melted the fat from the over-large belt lines and replaced lumps of fat with bulging muscles. The lanky and underweight, as I, took on from fifteen to twenty-five pounds, most of it going into broadening of the shoulders, hardening of arm and leg muscles. Prominent chest and flat stomachs were in style and much sought after by all the men. The sun's heat and the outdoor exercise added a healthy rugged tone to our facial complexion and strengthened the lines that led to the mouth and chin. Both the head and body posture went through a change that indicated development of physical power, firmness, determination and boldness; a fighting man's image.

We still lacked the finish and shine of the old timer, but that was understandable; it was the foundation we had been building, it was the rock bottom stuff we had been taking into our nature and physical structure. We had been building an addition to the Marine Corps. The rifle drills the firing range and all in the matter of weeks and we were tough and our individuality was in a sense gone. We were a disciplined machine; an order given would receive an automatic response. Though lacking in the professional killing skills, these were to come later in training in an advance course given at Quantico and France. We had reached the first goal of a recruit; we were automatons in the Marine Corps' machine.

The Marine Corps had copied and added to their own system some German methods that had proven successful in war. It was first tried out on Americans by a German officer who practiced his wares on General Washington's plowboy recruits. Excepting certain details, the German army dress uniform was similar in pattern to that of the Marines. The German belt buckle was decorated with the letters G.M. which when translated into English is "God is with us." Whereas the buckles worn by the Marines carried the letters U.S.M.C. which when translated into Marine lingo is : "US are Marine Corps." No kidding, the Marine pride in his Corps had no bounds. An individual Marine might admit that he himself was not so hot, but his company, his regiment and Corps, in his mind had no equal and he tries gosh-ding hard to prove it, whether on the parade ground or in war.

The Marine's tradition, the tales of adventure and valor, are not only passed from mouth to mouth around camp fires but are put to music and sung with vim and enthusiasm, almost with reverence, as *Till We Meet Again* is sung by our religious elders at their summer camp meetings. With all due apologies to all Marines for such a comparison, because I cannot at this time remember a more apt illustration. The Marine song calls to my mind the old war dance songs of the American Indians in which the Brave recounted all his personal victories against his enemies. The Marine song does just that.

The Marines have fought in many wars and have won many victories. So its history would fill many pages and when put to music and song make a hymn of more verses than the space allotted to it in this manuscript would allow. I will, however, give a few lines from the first and last verses of this hymn, which will demonstrate the nature of their song. Your imagination should enable you to visualize what a stirring scene it makes in the audience of a few thousand Marines singing this song:

> From the Halls of Montezuma,
> To the Shores of Tripoli,
> We fight our country's Battles
> On the Land as on the Sea.
> If the Army and the Navy
> Ever look on Heaven's Scene
> They will find the streets are
> Guarded by
> United States Marines.

While I personally never did get around to believing myself more than just an ordinary soldier, I did, as you probably have already guessed, get sold on the idea that a real Marine was a superior fighter. I never saw a Marine I wouldn't trust in a pinch, to risk his life to save another's. All my friends were potential heroes.

It is said that when ex-President Teddy Roosevelt was touring Europe that the Kaiser's generals put on a military show in honor of Teddy's visit. The Kaiser and Teddy were sitting together on the reviewing stand and after a magnificent show of military strength had passed, they were followed by a company of Marines led by the famous Marine band, and as they passed the reviewing stand the Kaiser was so thrilled with the perfection of their accomplished performance that in his excitement the Kaiser grabbed Teddy and said, "No other soldiers in the world could equal them for discipline and precision." He further said, "Only the German Army could produce soldiers of the perfection equal to them." Teddy, true to form, replied, "Shucks, Kaiser, those are my boys, they are United States Marines."

The daily routine of sameness had changed little since our first day's drill with our rifles, but as constant repetition of our movements continue, gradually these movements become a fixed habit and both mind and muscles react to a fixed rhythm that make things appear very different, and what once had been tiresome, painful labor had become a pleasure as our trained muscles no longer fight against each other in their clumsy response to orders. Now there were coordination and unity of muscular response that produce rhythm that not only takes drudgery out of the drills but adds an emotional thrill to the physical exercise.

Like small boys that Santa had given a new gun, we were anxious to try out our new rifles and see how well we could shoot. After a long and not always a patient wait our turn to use the rifle range came and we had an opportunity to bang to our heart's content. Our fun and aim for that matter was somewhat marred by the wind that came in with the tide and dust that followed in its wake. I did quite well during those periods when it was calm and the air was free of dust, but the wind and dust brought my average down and while I was aiming at a sharpshooter's medal, the best I was able to do was to rate a little silver bar with the word Marksman on it.

Well, my friend, tomorrow we hold our graduation exercise and as befitting a soldier's honored occasion, there is to be a parade, with the post band, a fancy bugle to call the play and the Post Commander and his aids to inspect and pass on our fitness to move up to high classes and advance courses offered at Quantico, Virginia. It will be my first time to mix with a larger group than the small training company. My first time to swing into company front and give an eyes-right salute to real military gold leafs and eagles. My first time to be under the direct command of a commissioned officer. Well, I didn't let 'firstitis' bother me one bit. I had gotten hold of some of that Marine self-esteem and with all that washing, brushing and polishing I had, done I felt that I could look a General in the eye and dare him to find any fault with my soldier image. Then too, the musical ring of that clear cut bugle call, and the thrilling march of the band sent shivers and tingling waves up and down my spine. As for keeping step, my feet and legs acted as if they were glued to the music and nothing could have separated them. There was magic in the air, and somehow my feet and legs recognized their master and followed the count without effort or thought. I was an automaton tuned to the right wave length, moving with the rhythm written on the sheets of the band's music. I couldn't go wrong.

It's over, the island's prison doors have opened for my departure. I have earned my freedom. I have served my time and we are bound for the second step on my trip to France and the war. It's good-by Parris Island and I admire and respect, honor and appreciate, and forever will be grateful for what you have done for me; for the thorough job you did on my body and the conditioning of my mind for the trials of war. Even so, I am happy to be on the move following the trail of my rainbow to its end and the pot of gold that awaits me there.

Your harsh treatment, your stern discipline and your relentless effort to make me ready for a cruel war was what I needed and what I got from you, for which I owe you a debt of gratitude and the memory of which I will ever be mindful of and ready to serve you to the limit of my capacity.

Chapter 4

Our journey to Quantico was by way of a luxurious Pullman, a treat that none of us had expected and wholly out of keeping with what we had been accustomed to in our daily lives. It was a realistic omen of what was to follow. We had made an upward step from a state of slavery on the prison island to one of civilized freedom and treatment. We never again were to be treated like lambs being prepared for slaughter. On this island one was treated as an outcast. He had no standing or recognition. He was neither a civilian or soldier. He was stripped of his civilian dignity and left hanging between two opposite poles, on the one side was his had-been civilian respected personality and on the other, not yet obtained dignity of a soldier.

After our graduation, we had a new status; we had moved up from the grammar grades to high school. Our diploma had carried with it privileges and a new dignity and respect that only earners of such a reward can appreciate. On the island, the petit corporal had all the brain for the training company, just enough to direct our every act and mood. In our new status we were put on our honor. Our nursemaid had been withdrawn. The discipline was still there but now it was more self-discipline and woe be unto the Marine who did not exercise it. On the island, we were told what to do and were punished if we failed to obey the orders. From now on we were supposed to know our responsibilities and the requirements that it took to meet them. It was no longer considered necessary to give us detailed instruction about, where and how to do the hundreds of little things that made for correct living. On the island we had a fence of restrictions around us. At Quantico there were very few physical barriers to our movements.

On the island one had to have a pass to go to such places as the post office or even church. At Quantico one could roam the country side and go visiting to such places as Washington, Baltimore, Philadelphia and New York City without pass or permit. On week-ends when holidays fell on Friday, anyone who had not drawn guard or other special duty could take off on Thursday afternoon and be gone until roll call the following Monday morning. The above was the general rule. There were, as a matter of course exceptions, but not too many. No doubt of it, more men were held on the base for lack of funds than because of military restrictions.

In military service parlance, only commissioned officers are addressed as gentlemen. On the other hand, in the sense of applying the term as meaning one who is in the possession of those standards of behavior that meet the demands of society for good conduct, every enlisted good man in the Marines was supposed to act like a gentleman while off duty and away from the base.

There were a lot of soldiers sent to France with no more training than we had received at Parris Island. I, indeed, came in contact with some in the trenches that had less training than we had received on the island and were less prepared physically to meet the exposure and hardships that they had to endure. But thanks to an established policy and good judgment of our Marine commander, we would be given more advanced training before leaving for France and the war. The advance training camp set up at Quantico was new and still in the process of development at the time I arrived there. The streets were still unpaved and after a heavy rain were so cut up by heavy supply trucks that they became a mass of churned up mud and water.

I had been assigned to and became a part of the newly formed Sixth Regiment which we all knew was to be sent to France as soon as the different battalions could finish their training and transportation was available to carry them across. We, as trainees in the Quantico school, might well be compared to high-school students who were definitely preparing for college and a job or profession at the end of their training. Quantico was our high school, our college work would be received in France, the war was our job. A battlefield was our goal, and any break or delay in our progress toward our goal was not to our liking and would be received with regret and disappointment. We were an egotistic bunch of men who believed that we could whip anybody and wanted an opportunity to prove it.

Preparedness comes first, but then, the underlying forces that makes a Marine a superior soldier are: he feels big, so acts big; he feels brave, so acts brave; he feels that he is good, so acts good. He knows that he is a part of a great tradition as a fighting soldier and not only must live up to that tradition as a group but himself make a contribution to it. They call it the Marine spirit. This spirit is the thing that makes a common soldier into a Marine.

One of our first lessons at Quantico was to learn the principles and know-how in the building of barbed wire entanglements. Anyone who has ever tangled with the barbs of a pasture fence knows what a tedious, prickly, mean business it is to handle the stuff. In France we would, if we were not darn lucky, be called on to string the stuff before our lines at night with the Germans only a few hundred yards away and if heard by them they would start their machine guns throwing bullets our way. Their fire in all probability would cause some trigger-happy boys on our side to start shooting off their guns. Then some nervous or curious party wanting to know what was going on in No Man's Land would start the shooting of rockets and star shells to light up the place and then ten-to-one the little one-pounder boys would begin dropping their shells out there. With these facts in mind you can realize the importance of learning the wire-entanglement business well and being able to handle the wire when it was too dark to be seen a hundred yards in the distance. Then too, there will be danger of bumping into some Germans on patrol who have come out in No Man's Land on their own business. One certainly won't want to start off a little war out there between the lines if it can possibly be avoided. When the two sides choose the same night to send patrols between the lines it becomes a risky business and it's not unusual for both sides to sneak back into their trench and call it quits for the night.

The second lesson on the subject of barbed wire entanglements was divided into two parts, one of which was how to pass through it hurriedly in the daytime when it didn't matter how much noise one made. Every one of us would, one time or another have to do that while someone was trying to kill us with bullets, hand grenades or shells. And many of us would see the day when all three of these deadly killers were coming at us at the same time. The odds are against you when you make the journey through quickly, and it means almost sure death if you are caught in the wire and remain stuck there for any length of time.

The other part of the lesson had to do with getting through the wire at night and cutting a passage way through it without making any noise. This required more skill than the first two, and the one most of us shied away from if there was an honorable way of getting out of it. However, the importance of knowing how to do these things was too great to let an opportunity to learn about them escape without making an effort to become efficient in performing these tasks.

Barbed wire entanglements were part of and went with trench warfare. While it was new in name and in several particulars, yet, as you may recall, in a lot of defense positions around Atlanta and other places the Confederate Army not only dug trenches but drove sharpened fence pickets into the ground in front of their positions. While the later defense measures of World War One looked considerably different from those of the Confederate days and were much more elaborate, their purpose was the same. Other changes were put into effect largely because of the improvement of the artillery and the necessity of keeping the men hid from the enemy. All of which resulted in the trenches becoming the field soldier's home a great part of his time; which also led to making them more elaborate and more livable.

It is possible that in the foreseen future all of the citizens of a country gone to war will sleep in trenches and dugouts, and come out only when necessity compels them to do so.

The trenches we dug during our training period at Quantico were very nice and built strictly according to given measurements and a drawn plan. The old trenches I lived in and fought from in France were in a more or less dilapidated condition. Like an old house, years of use and abuse had left them in a rather run down condition. By having been given some trench training at Quantico, we were not too ignorant of how to use them. However, we really had more use for foxholes than trenches for the type of fighting we engaged in. But we didn't get lessons on this subject until necessity forced it upon us. As I see it, the foxhole was America's most important contribution to World War One. Possibly I should mention and include the putting of poultry wire across wire entanglements which permitted our soldiers to walk across the wire, I didn't try this method of getting across the wire so can't vouch for it and personally doubt its efficiency in practice or the wisdom of its use.

When it became an accepted fact that the war was going to be of long duration, the Germans and the French began building elaborate trenches and dugouts. We captured some dugouts near the front lines that were equipped with electric lights and other luxuries.

Though our early training started off with the assumption that we in France would have to adapt our fighting to trench warfare, we refused to admit that it had to be a long drawn-out war, just moving from one trench to another. We talked and planned for what we called open warfare. We had to learn an awful lot of things under fire that could have very well been taught back in a training camp. We quickly learned under shell fire that one had to keep his body below the earth's surface and that a moving army could not leave it to the engineers and work crews to furnish the holes for the fighting men to crawl in.

Whether it was a squad of eight men or a whole company or army, fighting was a go and stop pattern of movements with the retreating side and those making the advance following the same general pattern. Which simply meant every time the fighting line stopped moving, it must have coverage and if it was not already there in the form of holes, ditches or trenches, the fighters must start digging their own holes.

When we moved up the Metz-to-Paris road to stop the German drive on Paris in the area, of Chateau-Thiery and the Belleau Wood, there were no trenches or ready prepared holes for us to occupy. We Marines were paired off by number from front to rear rank. One with a toy-like shovel, the other with a small pick. That's the way it was supposed to be, but not necessarily so; the tools did not always pair up like that.

There were no previous training or instruction on how to dig a two-man hole. Really none was needed, necessity took care of that when the shells began to fall. Common sense and self-preservation instincts took over when the emergency came. The shells started coming our way, the necessity for a hole was there, and we imme-diately began digging one long enough and wide enough for two people to lie sandwiched in, and if we had time some four feet deep. If we remained in the same place for only a short time, we left only a shallow hole and moved onto another location to claim the hole another had started in the new place or if none had been started, we settled down to the task of breaking ground for another hole.

To the best of my knowledge and recollection, I started and partially dug six of these holes the first night we went into Belleau Wood. Well, a fellow gets disgusted in time with so much digging and so much moving around and in my case on the above mentioned night I thought I had had enough digging and was sitting with my shoulder propped against a large sapling asleep when I was awakened by leaves falling in my face that had been knocked down by a small shell going through the tree top. I was sitting there wondering if I had better start digging me another hole but before I had made up my mind another shell came and this time hit the body of the tree some fifteen feet up. Then I moved over a few feet and started digging.

At Quantico, we went through a lot of bayonet drilling and became very efficient in the use of both the butt and bayonet end of the rifle. My Lieutenant was gifted with imagination and wasn't afraid to use it. He thought up and devised a boxing bayonet drill that not only gave us training in blocking an enemy's bayonet thrust, but included the know-how to disarm one by taking his rifle away from him.

When our platoon had gotten the bayonet-boxing drill down pat, it was decided that we were good enough to put on a public exposition of the drill without orders or music. To go with this we practiced up on going through the usual close order drills and manual of arms without orders or count, all in silence.

The Army and the Marines had a football game scheduled to be played in the Washington, D.C. stadium and it was arranged for us to perform between halves at this game.

The first half of our performance was pronounced, "Well Done Soldier," and drew cheers from the high and low ranking men in both the Army and the Marine section of the stadium. Before the cheering had died down from the first part of our performance, half of the platoon stacked their rifles and with the other half with rifles at fixed bayonets, we went back on the field and formed two lines. One line stood facing the other with their bayonets thrust forward in a charge position. The other, an unarmed line stood with their bare hands raised up and out. Then for several minutes there were moves and counter-moves of thrusts of the bayonet on the one side and the dodging, ducking, warding off the bayonet and dancing in-and-out movements of the unarmed group. Suddenly, the unarmed boys having succeeded in getting the men with rifles off balance with their rifles pointing upward, they moved in under their opponents' rifle barrel. Swiftly twisting their bodies in a left turn and at the same time grabbing the end of the barrel with their right hand and as the turn is completed, with their backs towards their opponent, the gun barrel is now across their shoulders making the barrel a lever. A downward jerk enforced by their body's weight, causes the rifles stock to fly upward and out of the hands of their opponent. The previous unarmed line is now in possession of the rifles and to add a little comedy to their performance chase their opponents off the field. Before you judge this to be a farce performance read what happened to a Washington cop, a true episode told in the following paragraph.

Later the same day, we were in the Pennsylvania railroad station waiting to board our train for Quantico. Our rifles were stacked and we were loitering on that broad long platform that separates the waiting room from the fenced tracks. Mingling with us were two large heavy Washington cops. While most of us were average to large men, one of our number was undersize and while he looked like and was called the Kid, he had whipcord muscles and was lightning fast in their use and he could hold his hand with men of much greater size. One of the cops thought he would have fun teasing our kid soldier and began ragging him good naturedly for associating with tough men and asked him if he wasn't the troops' mascot. The little fellow was used to being teased and took it good naturedly, but often turned the tables on his would-be tormentors. We had an idea that something surprising for the good natured cop was developing in the mind of the Kid. So the bunch watched with interest to see what would happen. We had an idea that the Kid would "pull" the cop's leg. Just how, we would wait and see. So it was not wholly unsuspected when he went to the stacked rifles and brought back with him a rifle and handing it to the policeman said, "With that thing I am able to kick as hard as the next one." The cop smiled, and suggested that the enemy would simply take the away from him. "Maybe so, but so far I have held on to it, and I don't want

37

you to let anyone take it away from you." "Well, don't worry son," said the cop, "people don't take things away from this cop." Before the last word was hardly out of his mouth, the Kid had gone into action. It all happened in one big flash of coordination of muscles and body and the Kid was standing there with the gun's stock held tightly pressed between his arm and his side and the barrel of the gun pointing at the cop's middle. The young fellow looked at the embarrassed red-faced, good-natured cop and said: "Now you take it away from me." The cop seeing how the Kid was holding the rifle realized that where that gun went the Kid would go, laughed and said, "No, son, you keep it."

Knowing how to disarm an enemy is something every soldier and policeman should know, and how to hold a gun so as to make it difficult for the other fellow to disarm you is of equal importance. And disarming a man is a dangerous business and one shouldn't try it except when it is the only reasonable thing to do.

I am ordinarily a practical careful person who does not take uncalled-for risks. Even so, I have had moments when I acted out of character and only good luck saved me from having to pay a heavy penalty for this laxation in the use of good judgment.

At the same time a soldier is trained to kill others, he is warned of the sure as hell fact that dire punishment will be handed out to him if he kills one of his own men. And to make sure he is careful how he handles his weapon, he is informed that accidents are inexcusable and that his weapons are to be fired only in the line of official duty.

The occasion for my reckless impulse horse-play was brought about and happened in a patch of woods where a large group of us were laying around, resting, playing cards and killing time in general. A special pal of mine had been sent off on a special mission and came up with a new belt loaded with ammunition and a new forty-five automatic. I started teasing him and in no time he was boasting of his gun toting ability. I boasted that I wouldn't be caught with that load hanging from my waist. One retort led to another and he raised the question, "What would you do if brought face to face with an armed enemy?" My boast was that, "I would disarm the bastard and kill him with his own gun," and proceeded to show him how it would be done, by disarming him. The safety was not on and the gun went off with a bang there in the midst of a crowd. Fortunately, no one was hurt, nor was there a witness other than our close buddies, and no one in authority learned about it. I had brought myself within a hair's-breadth of a serious court martial charge and what easily could have been the death of my best pal. I was indeed indebted and forever grateful to my good luck lady for saving me from my own impulsive and reckless act.

When we arrived in Quantico, I was attached to the Third Battalion of the Sixth Regiment. This regiment was being organized for service in France and we all knew it. The First Battalion was sent over in September and we knew that as rapidly as we could finish our training and there were available transportation, the different forces that made up the Sixth Regiment would be sent across. We learned on what we considered good grapevine authority that a Marine Transport carried all the Marines that were sent to France. I had figured that the transport would be ready to make the trip across in a couple of weeks plus a few days and applied for my rated ten-day furlough and pulled out for my first visit home since entering the service.

I had a nice time at home and made a point of telling my folks and friends that my battalion was making preparation to go across and that I would be on my way to France in a matter of a week or so.

Moving of troops, sailing, of ships and all transportation on the submarine infested ocean were a highly classified security secret during the war. Nevertheless, when I left my train from Georgia in the Pennsylvania railroad station in Washington and walked into the big waiting room, I immediately suspected that something was in the air. The center of excitement seemed to be associated with a bunch of Marines who were in a close compact group that had gathered in one corner of the station. Strolling over I asked, "What's the excitement about?" A question was shot back at me. "Haven't you heard the news? The Third Battalion of Marines is leaving for overseas early tomorrow morning." I already knew that there was no train I could take out for Quantico that night and had planned to spend the night in the city. Well, what could one do? After inquiring around, it developed that there were a dozen others in the same fix as I. The Third was also their battalion and no one wanted to be

39

left behind. It was further brought out that there was a non-stop special that would go through Quantico that was leaving in about thirty minutes. We quickly got together and designated one of our group to act as spokesman for all of us and the whole dozen went along with out temporary spokesman to the train master's office. We surrounded the official and our leader made his plea and argued that our furloughs were up at midnight and that our battalion was pulling our for France the next morning and that if we failed to report in before they left, that we would be court martialed as deserters and that he alone could save us from disaster by allowing us to board the special and put us off at Quantico.

After some argument, he reluctantly gave the necessary orders that permitted us to ride the special into Quantico.

While I do not know about the others, my mad rush to report back to Quantico and join my battalion was of no avail. I walked into my platoon's barrack that night to find the men giving the final touches toward being ready to pull out next morning at daybreak, and was greeted with, "You son of a gun, you are too late." Then more jeers and a horse-laugh. On reporting to the company's office, I was informed that I had been transferred to the 80th Company, Second Battalion Marines. The disappointment was triple in effect. My going overseas was put off until the Marine Transport could make another round trip and they were ready for us in France. I also regretted leaving my pals and the company.

While I was terribly disappointed at the time, as I look back I can see that my temporary loss was a longtime gain. The new group turned out to be just fine, and though it would be several months away before I could make it across, life in Quantico was much more pleasant than it would have been spending the whole winter in France, where fire, fuel and good food were not up to Quantico standard.

The moving picture industry was rapidly getting into position where it could play a great part in the nation's propaganda program. One movie was called, as I remember it, *What Price Glory,* but at the time this picture was being made no American soldiers were actually engaged in fighting in France. The American soldier's part in it had to be posed and was shot in this country. The rolling and open country near our camp was an ideal location and setting for the picture, and of course our Marine command was willing and ready to cooperate and have his men take part in this publicity stunt.

As for the men, it was their kind of thing ; they liked to show off; they went for it wholeheartedly. They were natural showmen and this was a chance in a lifetime for some of us to get into a live moving picture. It was something new, extra, and something to write home about. One fellow wrote home about being captain of the Head; his local paper got hold of the news and wrote a very complimentary article about the young fellow, told of his rapid climb in rank, and expressed its own and the town's delight in having a captain in the Marine Corps from their county.

You see we privates had to take turns in washing down, cleaning up and seeing to it that the toilets and other facilities in the washroom were kept in order; the day one was in charge, he was called Captain of the "Head." You can imagine what a laugh the gang had when that poor fellow's local paper found its way into our barrack. A fellow had to be a little careful what he wrote home; a lot of our letters found their way into the local paper.

All of us were in on the moving picture, so if one didn't go too far, he could get by with a lot of strutting and write home, "We are in the movies now, hot dog, ain't that something?" And with each letter home went directions for locating and recognizing their own boy or sweetheart by taking note of some specific object, section, shape of trees, and so on.

To us the making of the picture was a Roman holiday; we entered into it with spirit and vim. Very little of our activities were really posed in the sense of following a written individual script, though each individual did add his interpretation of his own part of the scene. It was in no sense of the word mob action. We were following planned maneuvers as in real fighting and had practiced them in our military training until we knew what to expect and in our imagination we could just about tell what to expect from the enemy. Down to the spot where one most likely would be killed. Some were due to be killed, some just wounded and some were to capture a German position and take prisoners. Everyone knew that the picture would sometime in the coming future be shown to the whole group and anyone who overdid his part would have the life teased out of him. The facts are that when the shooting got going we forgot all about the camera and had the feel of a real battle.

Most of us were given more than one part in the picture and were pretty sure that there would be at least one scene in which we could recognize ourselves. In one part, I was in a machine gun squad, in which I and another Marine were pulling a two-wheel, rubber-tired cart carrying a Lewis machine gun (which was never used by us in France). In another scene, I was fighting with a rifle with bayonet attached, charging the Germans down an incline. In this scene I was to be killed. When I reached a proper place to die, I pitched myself forward as one would when felled to the ground while running. As I fell I rammed my bayonet into the ground and let go. This left the rifle sticking in the ground with the butt standing quivering in the air, leaving a marker that stood there throughout the scene.

As you would guess part of the boys were dressed in real German fighting garb brought over here from France. During rest periods between scenes, we would make still camera pictures of each other in different poses, for our private records, and to mail out to our friends and home folks. While on liberty from camp we got a kick out of showing these pictures to civilians, and listening to their comments on how mean looking all the Germans were. A lot of them had seen the movie and were a little taken back to learn that the picture was made by us not in France, but in Quantico, Virginia. Nobody had told them that the picture was made in France, they had just assumed it.

Believe it or not, we Marines were not given the German hate propaganda treatment handed out to the civilians. Real, intelligent, loyal Americans do not have to have a heart full of hate to stand up for what they believe in, whether it be in war, religion, or politics. Hate is degrading and should not be indulged in as a substitute for loyalty, reason, understanding or convictions. Hate of war and evil of all kinds is justifiable, but blind hate is a poor weapon to use against anything and most assuredly will backfire against those that promote and use it to justify their stand or cause.

To us the war was a game, a rough game, in which the stakes were very high. So far as we could see, personal hate could very well be left out of it. There was one solid rule we fighters on both sides understood; if one side pulled a mean dirty trick there would be retaliation from the other. In war "You do unto others as they do unto you." To kill in hate is murder. To kill for personal gain is murder. A good soldier kills only when his duty requires it. Every young American should be drilled in these principles and our leaders told positively that it is not the loyal soldiers that kill on the battlefield but those that lead us into war. Those are the ones that one day will have to face the charge of having been a murderer.

A man can be a mean fighter without being a mean man, kill a dangerous body and still pray for the man's soul. Too many of our modern reformers and theologians don't seem to be able to understand the difference between killing for personal gain and in self-defense or for the protection of innocent people. It is the law of the land, the law of nature and the past history of God's written law that the guilty be punished and in proportion to the amount of the crime he has committed. Extreme crime calls for an extreme penalty. War to obtain an ambitious political goal is just as sinful as a war to obtain land or yellow gold.

Chapter 5

People who are proud of the show they make, which certainly includes the Marines (and about everyone else that has anything much to show), get a wonderful thrill out of parading before a large audience. And, of course, when the parade is routed down the historical Pennsylvania Avenue by the President's box in Washington, D.C., it becomes a grand thrill that makes it especially great. The occasion for this one was to boost the war effort and to add distinction to the new draftees throughout the nation. It is indeed, for any uniformed group, an unchallenged reward and distinguished privilege to keep step to the music of the greatest of them all, the President's own, the famous United States Marine Band.

The crowds were there in both number and quality. It was a military war parade, and we, the participants, were the nation's defendants in the hour of our country's need. We were soon to cross the dangerous waters of a broad ocean and fight our country's battles, some of us into death. The audience, many of them knew that from the ranks of these men were some who would give their all and have the dust of their bodies remain in the soil of a faraway land, and that there would be others who would return with their breasts covered with decorations for bravery and self-sacrifice. It was to some a serious sobering affair that brought tears to their eyes and a prayer to the lips and a dedicated resolve to never neglect, cease to appreciate or honor these men and others that would be following in their footsteps. To us in the parade came a spirit lifting cheer from the masses as we tramped our way down Pennsylvania Avenue.

How does one feel while passing in review before the President's stand, surrounded by all the top leaders of his country and the high brass of his own organization, and executes the salute? This is a difficult question for one to answer because he at that moment is in a kind of trance in which his emotional self dominates his body and soul. It is one of those occasions when his physical body is forgotten and his spirit takes over. It's a kind of detachment and his spirit seems to float along. At the moment of the salute a soldier is personally and in spirit symbolic of every thing his uniform, his Corps, his country and his flag stand for. It is a kind of spiritualism, an inner power that

44

few can fully understand and none can adequately describe. Any soldier who possesses this spiritual devotion to his country will give his life for it. A patriotic civilian holds his hat over his heart as the flag goes by to signify his respect and that his heart belongs to what his flag represents. The uniformed soldier's salute signifies respect and that not only does his heart and love belong to his country but that his life also is pledged for its safety.

The winter of 1917-18 is still remembered by people of my age and generation as a very cold one, and Quantico, Virginia did not escape its share of zero and below weather, with plenty of snow and ice. At that time somewhere above Quantico was located Indian Head, I believe it was called, a firing range for shooting and testing of artillery shells. These shells were aimed to fall down the river where they would land harmlessly in the water, not very far from Quantico. The river at this point, due to the backwater caused by Chesapeake Bay, is more than a mile wide. During that winter this river, the Potomac, was frozen over thick enough so one could have skated all the way to Washington and believe it or not one of the large shells, probably eight inches in diameter, fired from Indian Head landed on the ice in the river but instead of breaking through the ice, it ricocheted from the river and came to rest near our parade ground.

Our Red Cross Organization, through its appeal to our ladies and young girls, was able to supply us with wool knitted sweaters, mittens and scarfs. These articles of clothing gave us protection against the extreme cold nights while we walked our post on guard. With the thermometer registering four minus, the cold steel barrel of our rifle on contact with the bare fingers produced a torture very similar to handling red hot iron, and the nose also needed and received aid and some comfort, made possible by the Red Cross gifts. The lightweight, armless sweaters, worn under our shirts, most assuredly deserve mentioning of praise for the added comfort and warmth they supplied our bodies and I might add that they made many of the French girls happy to receive one as a gift.

It was the kind of night I would choose to be outside, so it was not a grievous disappointment to learn that I was required to leave the comfort of my home barrack and seat by the red, pot-bellied coal stove and go on guard at the reservoir, the source of the camp's supply. It was not a dangerous post. In fact, I had no live cartridges for my rifle and no one expected that I would be needing any. To some, it would have been a lonely, miserable assignment; not for me. I had my knitting, my heavy wool overcoat, imagination, and the love for the beautiful dreamy night, all of which accompanied me there and stayed to keep my body comfortable and my spirits warm and contented as the hours rolled by.

All the battalions of the Sixth Regiment but ours had already gone overseas, so ours had to be next to make the trip. There was very little fighting going on during the winter and no reason for rushing us across and according to our grapevine source of information we would spend the Christmas holidays over here. A few Marines had to remain on the post to do guard duty and take care of other routine matters connected with the camp's operation. Aside from that, everybody would be given about four days off. Not enough time for me to take a satisfactory trip to Georgia. So I sold my days to another soldier for ten dollars, which really meant that I would serve in the buyer's place on guard or other duties he might have been called on to do during the holiday period. As it turned out, I was restricted to the camp only one of the specified days and had the extra ten spot to spend on the three days I spent in a nearby city.

Chapter 6

I can't for the life of me remember the date, so let's say about, the middle of January, 1918, we left Quantico bound for France. We had had many inspections and all articles of clothing and equipment that was worn out, lost or in any respects unfit for we were ready to depart. Needless to say we were a jubilant bunch of men, for after all, we had for months been looking forward to this trip of going across.

It was late in January, while some of the Marines had gone over long ago and served as military police and one battalion of the Sixth Regiment had gone across as early as the previous September, we the tail end of the Sixth Regiment would soon join the Fifth Regiment of Marines and we with two army regiments, the 9th and 23rd infantry would furnish the infantry for the Second Division.

There was just one saddening incident to our leaving; one of our lieutenants would be left behind. The news had come to us that while at home on leave he had taken measles and would not be able to go across with his company. The very next time I was to see the lieutenant was at a bloody scene on a blood soaked road in France that was being shelled. I had seen the first shell being drop on a bunch of men who were carrying ammunition to the front and had joined some others to help get the wounded ones off the road and under cover. When I arrived on the scene, this lieutenant was in charge of directing the rescue work of the wounded.

From Quantico, we traveled by rail aboard a troop train to Philadelphia, where we went aboard the Marine Transport. This was my first trip of more than three miles away from my native shore. Whatever the reason, some said that the stabilizer was not working, others laid it to the rough January weather. To me it was rough and a never to be forgotten ride and only the desire to get back home could have enticed me to take another ocean trip. Probably the over-crowded condition and the location of my bunk was in part the cause of my discomfort. The foul air found below deck and the heating system were partly responsible. On some occasions, if one was on the top bunk, the hot air would almost roast him, whereas on other occasions if he was on the lower bunk he would come near freezing.

It seemed that there were no between freezing and roasting choice for one to take.

It took me some time to form the habit of holding tight to the sides of my bunk while I slept. However, I learned quickly to travel along the deck by a zigzag course of sliding from the high side to the low side of the deck as the ship rolled this and that way, up and down. The sailors ran the deck, but not me. My land-trained, gravity-conscious equilibrium would not function properly under the strain of the unaccustomed slants my body took or was forced to take by the ship's movements. Talk about sea legs all you wish; it was head and stomach trouble and not my legs that kept reminding me that I was a landlubber. I didn't get as sea sick as some of the others, but enough so as to develop a distaste for it and the high waves that caused it.

Our sea journey from Philadelphia to France was by way of New York City where we joined other ships that were being assembled there to make a convoy for the crossing of an ocean infested by German submarines. The water in the New York and off coast bay was covered with thick ice and it was so cold on the upper deck that I had no desire to idle away any time there.

Judging from the number of Marines called on to assist the sailors, it would appear that the ship was carrying only a skeleton crew. But since they had to make a return trip without our help, most likely they were holding out on us and taking advantage of an opportunity to make things easy and life more comfortable for themselves. It was quite obvious that the Marines had not been trained to perform many of the jobs assigned to them. The saying that good Marines are trained to do anything that comes to hand is only partially true.

They are taught self-reliance and are full of self-confidence. Two facts that enable them to learn quickly, and are willing to try to do any task assigned them. "I can't" has no place in their vocabulary and is never used.

In my rambles over the ship, I found Marines doing a great variety of things, but the one thing I was most thankful for having escaped was duty in the crow's nest. As you probably know, this observation post was called a crow's nest because like a real crow's nest it is about as far up in the air as one can find a place to build it. On land we would have called it a platform lookout or an observation post. The only way one could reach it or leave it was by way of a rope ladder, which, generally speaking, is something only sailors are adept at using to get up and down from high places. Then too, there is the matter of swinging back and forth out over the water as the ship leans this and that way with the roll of the ship as it slides into the deep troughs formed by high ocean waves.

Apparently all odds were stacked against it, even so my lady luck was along and saw me through. My assignment was in a small house placed on the main deck at the stern. I was on a submarine watch, with my post in an ideal location from which to look out upon the, to me, mysterious body of water. I just sat in front of a shelf like table looking out a window facing the ocean. The shelf was laid off in degree lines. Any object I saw in the water was sighted down a degree line and a corresponding reading was made and reported to the ship's bridge, through a speaking tube that was at my side. My orders were to just sit with my eyes watching the water and report any and everything that showed up in the area covered by my lookout.

Every section of the ocean was covered by at least two spotters and if one was slow in reporting an object in his area he quickly got a balling-out. We were plenty supervised and had to keep on the alert. This being my first trip into mid-ocean, I was far from being bored to death with my post. In fact I was delighted with it and would have been more thrilled than frightened if I had suddenly had a German submarine bobbing up in front of me.

We were approaching the European trail the German submarines followed in their journey from the Mediterranean Sea to their home base. Who knows, the word may have gone out that a whole fleet of submarines were in the area, and then, it might be that our newly arrived friends were just showing us a routine welcome to the European waters. Well, ours was a welcome committee and for us a happy one of small and large vessels, literally swarming in and out of our area around and between our line of vessels. They came at us at several times our own speed. They would come up close and then dot away like playing a touch and run game. The small speed boats reminded me of a bunch of bird dogs exploring a field for birds. They would run here and there covering the area around us as the dogs would, then they would seem to dash around a certain area as if they were getting the scent of a submarine and then light out on a mad run to some distant point, then whirl around and come hurrying back, mingle with the convoy, dancing around in and out of our line of march, They created the image of a bird dog seeking for the scent of hunted game, the grace of greyhounds as they dashed across the race lines, the enthusiasm of a pet house dog as it bounces around its master. It was all there: fun, sport and play, business, good nature and war-like seriousness. After recovering from our seasickness we had raving appetites and only two meals each day left our stomachs in an unsatisfied empty condition.

Our inability to get fresh or saltless water should be added to my complaints. Like food it was rationed in little portions that got smaller and smaller until none was left for the latecomers. Then the meat, that meat, some said it was horse meat, others said it was whale meat; whatever it was, I don't want any more of it. It had a sickly, pale red color after it supposedly had been cooked and tasted awful. It looked, smelled and tasted disgustingly raw.

Along about the third day out from New York in my rounds over the ship, I inhaled a delicious odor floating through the air. The central station where my nerves made their report diagnosed the odor as coming from newly baked bread just being lifted from a hot oven. But how was I to get in possession of a loaf of that bread? The idea of a Marine begging for bread from a sailor was unthinkable; stealing from him was different, even commendable at times, but in this case was too dangerous to try. For a sailor's brig is no place for any Marine to be.

The six cent loaf cost me twenty-five cents. Of course, no one was supposed to sell it, but such things are often done. Our deal was a very simple one. I would catch a time when no one who might be concerned about such matters were around to see the transaction, walk up to the bakery window and place a quarter on the window shelf, then the baker or his assistant would place a nice, fresh, warm loaf of bread by the quarter. I would pick up the bread and hide it under my blouse, at the same time the baker's assistant would pocket the quarter. All of which was done much quicker than I can write.

50

I had begun to feel the need of a bath. I gathered up my fresh-water soap and bath towel and started out to take my first shower on a sea going ship. To put it mildly, the more I tried to lather my body in the usual way, the stickier my body got and in the end I left the showers feeling that I would have felt cleaner and been better off without my bath taken under the cold, sea water showers. Later I found that bathing becomes more satisfactory when salt water soap was used.

Chapter 7

France, the Marines have arrived. I would like to weave my way along the narrow canal with dramatic words and gestures, and approach Saint Nazaire's docks beside the railroad siding with drawn swords and resounding clanking armor and bring back to life the knights of old. But as we got closer to the battlefields of a modern war, one is brought face to face with the fact that this was no dream war of knightly contest between noblemen, but a real war in which art, drama and love have no chance of survival in the mad rush to kill and destroy everything found in the path of an advancing army.

The quaint old cobblestones that surface the streets to the base of their homes were soiled with human and animal droppings and I personally witnessed one old lady squatting in the streets. It is true that the people, as they received word that our ship was coming into their neighborhood, emptied their houses and filled the streets along the route beside the canal. But no one greeted us with shouts of joy. Their burden of poverty and other ills of war left no room in their hearts for joy. The loud tramp, tramp of their wooden shoes as they chased after our slow-moving ship, the pitiful conditions of their clothes and the entreaty of their hands as they raised them to arms' length to catch any gifts the soldiers lining the ship's deck would pitch them and the eagerness with which they scrambled for the small coins that escaped being caught and fell upon the dirty cobblestones vanished any lingering dream of a land of ancient romance.

Thus in truth, I entered France. Dirt and filth had spoiled the earth. It was no more inviting now than the angry rough tumbling sea waves. I just didn't have the heart to let my mind pry into or speculate about these people. Apparently, on the surface at least, these people had lost their pride and self-respect along with their wealth and near kin.

Instead of shouts of joy, we gave a sigh of relief as our ship was docked. Our hearts were heavy laden with sorrow for these destitute people. It was pitiful beggars we had come to save. Before the orders came to board our assigned dinky little French train of cattle or horse cars, we were informed that we would spend the whole night and longer in our horse car and that where we were going it would be very cold and that during the night it would get real cold in our car. Only the ranking officers were given passenger coaches. Our car was labeled, "Eight Horses or Forty Men." The floor of our car was covered with clean straw. While it didn't smell too strongly, one could tell that it had stabled horses not so very long ago in the past. The Marines averaged larger than the French soldiers. Anyway, we squeezed in forty strong with our sixty pound packs, rifles and a lot of extra luxuries that one likes to take along (I had a few books I had selected to read while overseas).

Before leaving Saint Nazaire, a large brand new American garbage can was put aboard our horse car. This can was to be used as a catch-all storage place. In it went our empty cans, cracker boxes and other litter. There would be practically no food to find its way into it. Our travelling rations were always for some unknown reason very meager and never quite enough to satisfy one's appetite.

It took only a few minutes for the Marines to get aboard the train and we were on our way to that part of France that is chilled by cold air that sweeps down from the Swiss mountains. We had settled down as best we could in the overcrowded car and had already begun to wonder what we could do to relieve the monotony of our slow ride across France when our train pulled on a siding in a small town leaving our car standing across from a station platform on which was a large size barrel of white wine. Two husky Marines eased out of the car and seeing no one was looking their way, quickly moved the wine to a place inside our car. As the train pulled out from the village the drum top was removed and we all got set for a drinking party.

There was no discussion, no orders were given for none were needed, because everybody was of the same mind, they all wanted a drink. There was no rush, no attempt to push or shove, it was apparent to all of us that there was plenty for everyone to get his fill and some to spare. Though no words were spoken on the subject, I am pretty sure that it was in the minds of each that we would have a night-long party since there was little chance of a comfortable place for one's body to lay down and sleep. Why not take it easy and drink in leisure and enjoy the stuff as it trickled down our throats? No one in our crowded car dreamed of the possibility that our treasure might be snatched away from us. So as the sun was sinking lower and lower toward the hills in the far away west, we began to dip our canteen cups into the sparkling liquid, smacking our lips in demonstration of our approval of the drink. I am pretty sure that none of us had ever come in contact with French white wine previous to this occasion. As for me, I thought it was apple cider fermented differently from any I had ever tried.

We were enjoying ourselves, the party was progressing nicely and our bodies didn't seem as tired or restless as an hour previous. There were no drooping eyelids or other indications of drowsiness nor did our instincts give us any warning that danger was lurking. Then the word was passed down the length of the long train from the officer's coach that someone had stolen a barrel of wine and that it was suspected that the wine was on our train and that the train would be held up and searched when we arrived at the next large town. "Now who but a blank-to-blank Frenchman would wire ahead, hold up and have searched a whole troop train for the sake of one lousy, measly little keg of wine?"

We got busy and removed all the litter from the garbage can and the wine from the barrel was poured into it. Then as the train was passing through a thinly populated country section, the empty wine barrel was pitched from the traveling train and went rolling down an embankment that stretched out from the tracks. A game of cards was started, so when the search was on for the missing barrel the stage was all set and a card game was in progress with a ring of fellows encircling the garbage can in our car. There were small piles of kitchen matches, a common substitute for money, placed at the proper place on the can's lid and cards were being dealt and discards made to and by the players around the can. Ours was a long train and the time allotted for the search was short and our train officer didn't want the stolen wine found on his train. So when our officer and the French official arrived at our car, our officer greeted us with, "Carry on." The game continued as if everything was normal. The French officer let his eyes roam over the car and saw nothing to arouse his suspicion, nodded his head as if to indicate to the Marine officer that it's not in this car, and they passed on.

There are no drunks as yet but most every one seems to be at that stage of intoxication when it is fun just to be alive and the most reserved of them raise their voices for all to hear and actually admire the noise that comes from their own throats. Everything is fun and all are jubilant and there are no cross-tempered, ill-mannered jerks in our car or group. The night rolls on with fun, laughter and song as voices go ringing into the night's darkness, and only at long intervals does an outside noise break into the party's glamour. And then it is the long, lonesome wail of our locomotive's steam whistle that comes back to us as she passes between two hills and the engine's voice seems to bounce back and forth as if hunting for its way out of the railroad cut.

As we travel on headed toward the rolling hills of eastern and north France, the air grew chilly and then really cold. Many a soldier on that train pulled his blanket tighter around his shivering body and struggled to warm himself. Not me, not us, in our car because we had the alcoholic fire from the garbage can burning within our bodies and like any alcoholic burner it sent warmth through our bodies and kindled our spirits. For hours without letup, we drank. We said toasts to ourselves, the garbage can, to France and the war.

It was a healthy, reckless young bunch, but too much is more than anyone can take. So one by one they began to drop out in a drunkard's stupor and the power of the wine's kick was on the wane. Some fell asleep and lay in a tangled mix-up of legs, arms and bodies with no conscious knowledge of their positions or condition of themselves. It was more than some stomachs could stand. There was vomiting in the car where men were packed like fish in a sardine can. I was warned by signals from my stomach and had closed my own canteen cup and did not take the one too many. I soon descended in spirits from the top of the world, down from the warm, comfortable, jolly spirits sustained by an alcoholic stimulant and was now chilled and sunk beneath layer after layer of miseries. And with each newly added slobbering, vomiting, messy, drunken victim of the garbage can my disgust heightened and my miseries became more embarrassing and more intolerable. I was as low in the dumps as one can get and still retain self-control and a semblance of sanity.

I was humiliated, disgusted and trapped; there was no escape from it. I had to take it. Apparently, I was the only sober man in a tight wad of forty men. The odor in the closed car, the slimy disgusted sight and feel, with only candle light, was and is too much for words and too unpleasant to think about.

Where we were going, and where we would be, there were no culture centers or other planned entertainment for American troops. These luxuries were to follow in time, but for now and for months to come they would halt farther south and east and beyond our reach and be absent from our sector. We had following us a Y.M.C.A. young Methodist preacher who tried his best to keep up with us carrying his sale's pack, which was mindful of the old days when country walking peddlers made their rounds through the rural sections carrying a heavy pack strapped to their back. The Y.M.C.A. pack contained cigarettes, chewing gum, candy bars and thin writing paper in contrast to the old peddler's wares of calico cloth, thread and other articles needed by country housewives.

This young preacher was a good scout. On Sunday morning, as on other days, he would open his pack and sell his wares to tired soldiers passing his dugout door to and from the advance trenches. It was a Memorial Day to me when I traded him a woolen blanket, which he needed badly, for some cigars. It hurt my conscience to accept pay for the blanket but he insisted on me taking them. As it turned out, these were the first and only cigars I would puff in my eleven months' stay in France. If he is still alive, it is very likely that he remembers the blanket as I remember the cigars. Little things like that often stick in one's memory when real big things are totally forgotten.

As the young preacher said one Sunday morning, "What would my devout people back home think if they could see me trafficking cigarettes and not leading some bunch of men in prayer this Sunday morning?" Well, at that time we combat troops in my division had very few opportunities to replenish our supply of tobacco and this young preacher knew it and believe it or not, our physical needs were our chief concern and personal contact with one who understood our situation and went through the hardships this young preacher had to suffer to serve us contained a spiritual value that penetrated through and became a part of every transaction he made. To my way

56

of thinking, his service was his sermon, his feelings for us his prayer and the quiet conversations he had with us when the opportunity presented itself spoke louder than any formal sermon would have done.

Chapter 8

A night and day has gone by, so has all the wine, and the foul odor and the mess. A thorough job of cleaning and policing up has taken place and as we roll into a small railroad town a mile or so from our final destination, all the men have sobered up and are back in normal condition and everything is as if the party had not taken place. This train journey is just another incident in a busy Marine's life. Like a dream, with a mixture of glory and nightmare, they come, they go – today is here and tomorrow is on its way.

We left our train and marched over to a small village where we would spend February and about two weeks of March. Here we would turn in our American Lewis machine guns and were issued some French automatic rifles to take their place and also receive some outmoded French gas masks that we would use until we received our issue of American masks. We were soon to learn that our idea of a warm France with lots of beautiful French girls was a fantastic dream that didn't in any way approach reality for a long time. At first one wondered where all the girls had gone. Apparently the only women folk left in the dozens of small villages were old, weather-beaten, field-worked, tired and worn-out women that had as much romantic appeal to us young fellows as an old shoe.

The one exception, in my experience, was the young widow of a French officer. She had looks, poise, education, culture and two bright children, a boy and girl of six and seven years of age. I enjoyed her friendship and was delighted with the children. We would play school and I would read and translate into English their child readers. They laughed at my French pronunciation, but because the children had fewer and easier words in their vocabulary than their mother I found that I could carry on a conversation with them with greater ease than I could with their mother. In some cases when I couldn't pronounce a word I would write it and the children were amazed that I could write, but, as the children put it, "couldn't talk it."

The family lived in the front part of the home. In the back was a large basement walled in room where we had our company's kitchen and where we gathered when shells were dropping nearby. Above

58

this was an attic where a pal and I had selected to sleep. The children to my surprise were not frightened the few times that shells fell close by. The Germans were quite a distance away and could shell the place only with their long-ranged guns, and really did not shell the town as they did those near the front. Their target was a bridge across the river several hundred yards below us. I don't remember for sure but believe there were both a vehicle and railroad bridge down there. Apparently our house was in the path of the shell aimed at the bridge and those that fell near their target passed directly over our attic room and would already be on their downward journey as they went past us. Falling shells made a different noise from one not turned downward.

Late one night the Germans seemed more determined than usual to destroy the bridge and about every fifteen or twenty minutes would send over another shell. For a while every time a shell came over my pal would say, "Hemrick, let's go down." Each time I would say, "Hell no! Those Germans are not going to miss that bridge this far." My pal after a time fell into a sound sleep and was not awakened by this one, which came so close that it made the whole attic shake as it whizzed by and hit the ground so close that the rocks and pieces from the exploded shell that were blown high in the air rained down on the roof above my head. Gosh, if that miss had been a couple of feet lower the concussion alone from that size shell would have been enough to have blown that roof and us in the attic into smithereens. Well, it seemed that I had overestimated the accuracy of one German gunner, and was fumbling around in the dark for my clothes when my pal awoke and asked, "What's you doing Hemrick?"

"Time to go down pal," was my reply. "Those darn Germans have begun to miss this far."

In the village we moved into, our platoon was bunked down in a barrack that did not have any bunks. Instead it had a platform slightly higher than the dirt floor and which ran the entire length of the building. We spread our blankets on this platform and slept there. The bunk house had one small wood stove. We had snow and ice and some real cold weather during the month of February. We had a small amount of wood issued to us for our stove, but not enough; so when we ran short we did some night foraging for wood.

I remember seeing one of the fellows coming in with what looked to me like some farmer's barn-shed door on his broad back.

One Sunday an opportunity presented itself and we made a real haul. It was like this: Our platoon was taking a single-file cross country hike and came by a sawmill with several stacks of lumber piled almost directly in line with our walk. The sawmill was closed down for the day and no one was at the site. The first man in line as he passed the lumber shouldered a plank, each man in line in turn did the same as he passed the neatly stacked pile of lumber. Thus we arrived at our barrack with fifty odd planks.

We knew that on the morrow the lumber would be missed and that some indignant French manager would start yelling, 'American soldats' have robbed his beloved France of its most precious lumber. Such serious charges could not be ignored, and a search for the lumber would be made. While it is generally understood that soldiers take whatever action that is necessary for their survival, the universal rule is, "Don't get caught." Government officials from the president down and all good politicians practice this philosophy of "Don't get caught." Our officials knew that we were not getting enough wood but there was little they could do about it, and while they never could officially admit that there was stealing going on, they knew it, and what's more they did not object to it as long as we were not proven guilty. The French furnished less wood than they got paid for so we stole to square the accounts.

As we had expected, early Monday morning the angry, excited French sawmill manager arrived, and our barrack was searched. Fifty planks make quite a lot of lumber and it could be a big problem for most people to hide it in a twenty by sixty foot bunk house. Even so, and it was all there, not a splinter of it was found. Marines are smart guys you know, and our best officers have good poker faces.

Generally, we Marines are kept too busy to do much loitering around, and yet there were a few hours each day when one was free to plan his own entertainment. I was a poor card player and had no desire to gamble, which was the most common source of pleasure in the group. Next on the list of pleasure was wine and beer drinking. While I liked the taste of the two drinks sold in the village shops, I did not cater to the crowded, boisterous, sometimes drunken atmosphere of some places where drinks were sold. Not all, of course, were like that and sometimes a few of us moderates would get together and play a few hands of cards with one dime as the limit anyone could bid. Tiring of the game some of us might tour the village, going in and out of the different public places taking a few drinks but never enough to become intoxicated.

I had newly discovered and became interested in the quaint, many centuries old village cemeteries of rural France. With me it became a hobby to search out these places and ponder over the historical facts and to take a special note of the difference between these and our cemeteries back home. Naturally, it followed that my letters often carried descriptions of these visits to the different churches and their walled cemeteries. After a time information came back to me that someone had censored my letters and deleted so much of my letters' contents that there was little left but the heading and the closing remarks. I was puzzled and disgusted. I could not figure or imagine why my letters were so thoroughly stripped of their content. I had made no remarks that could in any way be associated with the war or its secrets. It was later, by putting together tiny facts gathered here and there, that I arrived at the conclusion that some psychiatrist had read my letters and come to the conclusion that I was mentally unbalanced by fear of the approaching death I was expecting and that my people back home would reach the same conclusion. How ridiculous! In my silent anger, I resolved that from then on no censor would be stripping my letters if I could figure a way to outsmart them.

Back at headquarters, we had a good, kindly, Catholic soldier's chaplain. Along with his religion he possessed all those good human traits of a Father and a soldier. He was human. He was a brave man, possessed humor, could and did work tirelessly with his hands when the need called for it. I did not know him personally, but when a bunch of Marines are unanimous in their praise of anyone, there is no doubt in my mind and needn't be any in yours about his rating at the top in any standard of grading one may choose to use. I was told that one time during our heavy fighting there were not available men to bury our dead and the good Father would lay his bible aside and help with the pick and shovel work. On one occasion, while he was covering the body in a quickly dug grave a shell exploded nearby and pieces from it cut off the end of the Priest's shovel handle. He looked up in surprise, went over and picked up the part of it that had fallen a few feet away, carried it tenderly and laid it in the grave by the body, picked up another shovel, smiled at those present and then proceeded with the work of covering the body and the end of his shovel handle. Among other things he did, over and above the call of duty, he would censor a soldier's outgoing letters. And as if he understood that one would want to write some things he would not want read by a censor and so mark the letter and envelope and hand it back unsealed for the soldier to mail. This gave the soldier an opportunity to write in some special message of a private nature.

It happened just a short time before we were scheduled to move out headed for the battle front. I was ordered without explanation to report to the doctor. There were many soldiers there to see the doctor, who had a deadline in which to finish his inspection of the men. There was no time for the consulting of the men's medical records or for a detailed questioning of all men reporting to him. As I was advanced in the line toward the doctor, I learned the general purpose of the inspection was to weed out those men who were unfit for trench service and that the doctor was too busy and had too little time to give more than a quick glance at, and to put no more than one or two questions to each man. It appeared to me that if a man was slow in answering or seemed in doubt as to why he was there the man was shifted to a table and a more detailed study was made of his case, and some were immediately transferred out of their company. The thought struck me that I had been left behind once, and be-danged if I would let it happen to me again. So when I faced the doctor I was ready for his snappy question.

"Why are you here?"

My answer was, "Doctor, last week I had the bellyache, it's well now." The doctor, as I had expected he would, ordered me back to my company.

Shortly after this took place, zero hour had arrived and we were in formation with all of our worldly goods, ready to hike over to the railroad town and station where we would again board a little dinky train. This time we would ride the train up as near the front as they dared run a troop train. Before the orders were given to shove off, our platoon lieutenant walked down the line giving his men the once-over and spied me in the ranks. He came over to me and said, "What are you doing in there?"

"Doctor's orders, sir, he ordered me back to my company," was my reply.

The lieutenant, with a puzzled look on his face, hesitated for a few seconds and then said, "Well, O.K.," and passed down the line. In soldier's language, "Hot dog, I've made it." Whether it was my feet that had given me trouble, or a suspiciousness of my sanity, or it could be possible that they had other plans for my future, I can never be sure which. Whatever the reason, my lieutenant was an honorable man and I do appreciate the good intentions of my officers of whom I have no complaint. I freely admit that few if any of the other Marines preferred to visit historical cemeteries to the local wine shops, or to sit on a ridge and gaze at the beautiful rural scenes that adorned the lowlands to that of sitting around a card table. All of which did, in a way, make me an oddity.

Dog gone it, why can't our civilian bosses realize that if the boys were encouraged to write what they pleased about themselves and what they were doing, there would be a lot more boys anxious to get in there and make heroes of themselves?

Take me. Back there I could see in my imagination my girlfriend rushing out to meet the R.F.D. man as she saw his old grey horse pull up beside the family mailbox. And my brothers making a special trip to the post office to get and read my latest dispatch of my part in the war. In the secret recess of my mind, I was in rebellion against all censorship. My people had sense enough to know that the war was no picnic. The chances were ten-to-one that they would worry much less if they knew the real facts as given to them direct by word from me than if they heard nothing.

There was only a small chance for one to do any constructive thinking in a freight car jammed with thirty to forty noisy men. However, on this trip there were two escapes from the crowd. Our car had a tiny super-structure, very small and a little uncomfortable to ride in, otherwise similar to the cabooses of the American freight train. The second chance was a flat car hooked onto our car and which was loaded with the battalion's equipment, such as water carts and rolling kitchen stoves. Between the different objects and under the two wheeled carts and other wheeled vehicles were many places where one might sit and rest in comfort. I quickly discovered and used these places from time to time to retreat to a place to meditate and write my letters.

Every trip has some minor incidents that linger in one's memory, though they are not of great importance, they do help to betray a war picture that is not found in school books. Food and drink rank with gun and ammunition in importance in any fighting soldier's thought. The fact that I was able to purchase a fresh-baked, warm loaf of French bread during this trip, and thus had a judicious appetizing supplement to my meager portion of corn beef hash and soda crackers that made up our traveling rations, was of paramount importance to me. Then, during the cold hours of the long night, when we were, called from our car to be served by a Frenchman with hot black coffee spiked, as was a French custom, with a shot of rum. All things considered, these things deserve a place in my memories of the war period.

A more like war incident was our train's narrow escape being caught in a German air raid. As it happened, our train was halted just outside the railroad junction and held there until the bombers were driven from the place. In my lookout from the super-structure I was able to watch the raid that took place in the railroad junction town. It was just fine that one of the bombers did not come flying down the track and drop one of their bombs on the middle of our train. A bombing raid is an interesting sight if you are far enough away to be out of danger. In fact, if you are in the target area you don't see it at all because in that case you will be in a dugout if one is handy and if there are no dugouts at hand you will be laying flat on the ground behind any protection available. To use a guess, I will say that had we been ten minutes earlier we would have been in the middle of that raid and not just an onlooker.

From my watchtower on our car, I noticed numerous large crosses that were placed here and there along our train's route. These crosses denoted the spot where some plane had crashed with its dead pilot. They furnished proof to me that we were traveling through a dangerous section that was subject to constant air raids and dog-fights between the Germans and our forces. I have no recollection of where or when, or the time of day it was when we left the train and started on our hike to our final destination. It is possible that a touch of night-blindness was affecting my eyes at the time for I do remember that before we arrived at the new home I could not see the man marching at my side and bumped into him constantly. No question about it being a dark night, but not as dark to the others as it was to me, for if it had been we could not have found our way to the bunk house where we entered and spent the rest of the night and where we would remain probably a week or more.

The bunk barrack that housed my platoon was small for the men crowded into it. The bunks were built in units of four spaces for four men, with two upper and two lower spaces for a total unit of four. It was a simple frame work seven by four feet with wire netting stretched across the frame's railings. There were two other rows of these running the entire length of the building. There was a wide double door at the front that stayed open and was used for all entering and departing from the building. I do not know about a rear end door, for I never went to that end of the barrack. I do not recall how many men were crowded into this small building.

The next day the German artillery dropped a dozen or more shells at a watering place a few hundred yards below our bunk house. This led me to wonder about the possibility of having a gas shell make a direct hit on our house during the night while all of us were crowded asleep in our bunks. The mental picture of all those men suddenly awakened with the sounding of a gas alarm and all knowing that mustard gas confined to that small room could be disastrous within only a few minutes exposure to it!

The thought almost gave me a case of the shivers and caused me to give some thought to the problem of getting out. My bunk was just a few feet from the door, so I planned how to reach it without getting into the main aisle which I judged would be packed with human bodies and should one be knocked off his feet he could very well be trampled to death. My plans of escape made, I felt secure in my own survival and dismissed any further thought of gas from my mind.

It had been a hard day for the men, and now they were relaxed and sound asleep. It was a cool, still, quiet night with hardly a breeze stirring, an ideal night for effective use of gas shells. It was pitch dark in there and all of them were asleep.

Suddenly the silence of the midnight was broken by the loud, frightful cry, "GAS!" The great mass of men were jarred to wide awakeness and instantly, even before the ring of that feared cry had died out, hands begun scrambling for gas masks and a jumping, scrambling, pushing mass of human bodies were trying to wedge their way into that dark hidden narrow aisle. An alert guard stationed just outside a few feet from the door who himself had been jarred to action by the cry instantly realizing what the reaction of the men inside that crowded room would be and realizing the danger, leaped for the door and yelled at the top of his voice, "FALSE ALARM!"

The scramble to get out ceased, men began to feel their way back to their bunks. The scrambling mass of humans quickly calmed down, and slowly felt their way in the darkness to their bunks. Then the inevitable question arose, "What blank to blank son of a gun idiot gave that alarm?" It was no time for the wicked to confess his sins. There was no way to trace down the guilty party. So things soon quieted down and the bunch went back to sleep and the unsolved mystery of the false gas' alarm was soon forgotten and probably remains a forgotten episode in the minds of all but the person who gave the alarm. Well, it was I. I was having a nightmare and interrupted my own sleep with the cry and being the first to awaken was the only witness to the crime. Just another case when my good luck was all that could have saved me.

While my platoon never suffered the misfortune of having a gas shell land on its bunk house, one platoon in my regiment did suffer such a tragedy and while I did not witness it I was told that a number of men were so blinded by the gas that they had to be led by the hand to the ambulance that carried them to a hospital.

I suspect that at one time or another all of us were exposed to and got more gas than was good for us. At one time I thought it was gas that made me sick at my stomach. From what I have heard and read my platoon suffered less from gas than many of the other outfits; so far as I know none of the men in my platoon ever suffered seriously from gas. A lot of times it was due to carelessness that led to being gassed. Wearing our gas mask while marching from one location to another was so disagreeable that we did not wear it even when we had reason to believe that there was gas in the low places along our route.

At the time I was assigned to the chow detail, only the mess sergeant, two cooks and assistant cooks were kept back in the rear when our company moved up to hold front line trenches or to make an attack upon the enemy. So that while there were advantages in being attached to the kitchen detail, it also had its disadvantages and very few men ever sought after a job in the kitchen. The usual procedure was to join and go up to the fighting line with the company and remain with it and sleep in the trenches along with the men and join in the fight should there be an attack. Otherwise, we had no trench duties except the early morning watch at which time everybody was alerted and stood watch. Our specific job was to do what we could to get food to the men in the trenches and on the line. Thus when things were quiet on the front, I was boss of my own time, free to move about pretty much as I pleased. I could volunteer for such things as came to hand. My special required duty was to see to it that the men got their chow. Not too many men liked this dual kind of service. It suited me just fine because it permitted me to roam around and go places, and be pretty much on my own. I took my required duties seriously, and was never caught abusing my privileges. In all, it added up to me having had a greater variety of experiences and a broader view of what was going on than the average soldier in the ranks.

At the time I joined the kitchen force, a sergeant friend of mine had recently been made mess sergeant and he made me bread man. My job was to slice the bread with uniform thickness that would allow two slices for each man with a minimum of a couple of loaves left in case we had latecomers. This was a much nicer job than some others connected with the kitchen work.

I was able to find a Frenchman who had a hand grinding stone and I put a keen edge on my foot-long bread knife. It was my belief that the sergeant gave me the responsibility of the bread because he thought I would do a better job of it than the others. (That everyone got the same thickness bread is important when each of the two hundred and fifty men are wanting a little more than he is getting and is watching closely for evidence that the other fellow is getting more than he). And if the bread were to give out before the last man in the chow line reached the bread table that guy would have been plenty mad and ready to beat hell out of the bread man.

There were many times when the men got less than their stomachs wanted and the men would kid, flatter, argue, just anything he could think of, that might get a little extra food on his plate. Through it all I tried to be absolutely fair and was as hard as nails when the occasion called for it. A new captain to our company after listening to how I managed the hungry men while dishing out their chow was so impressed that he took me to be the mess sergeant for a short period I acted in that capacity.

We were issued a small amount of sweet raisins and nice choice dates that made a soldier's mouth water and were something that most soldiers would steal if given half a chance. I immediately put them under lock and key and let the kitchen crowd know that none left my hands until I was ready to issue them to the whole company. Well, the whole crew from head cook down was sore at me until the whole thing was forgotten. Naturally, the kitchen gang thought I was stuffing on those goodies while they had to wait around until I had time to count and figure and give each of them their 250th part and meager share of the goodies. The army issues rations on the basis of what an average soldier should eat under average conditions. The Marines were larger and more active than the average soldier so quite often we were not issued as much food as one really needed. At one time we had in my squad what we considered an under-size corporal. He ate less than most of us. Also in the squad was a tall, extra broad-shouldered man that was as strong as a horse and would, when he could get it, eat fully as much. It was a common practice of this corporal to remove something like a third of his grub into the mess kit of our Big Boy, as we called him. Fellows like this one would go back for a second serving when food was plentiful, but in our company too often there was no food left from the first serving.

Anything sweet was a treat to our men, they just couldn't get enough. We did occasionally get syrup issued in gallon cans but there were times when we got the empty can after someone along the route had removed the syrup from it.

Somewhere our cook had learned how to mix a batter of canned milk and sugar, dip a slice of bread in the batter and then drop it into a pan of boiling grease. This produced what to us was a most delicious toast. We hadn't had any of this toast in a long time and I felt like giving the men a treat. In a diplomatic way, I got talking to the cook about his famed French toast. In the end it was decided that if I would see to the bread and sugar he would see to the rest. At that time our sugar was almost gone, but I was sure some company cook somewhere in the camp had, by some hook or crook, an over-supply on hand and I set out to find it.

In the second or third company kitchen I tackled, I found the sugar and began to bargain the mess sergeant for its possession. By putting up as collateral a ten dollar gold certificate of mine, I managed to borrow a fifty pound sack of sugar and by slicing their bread a little thinner a couple of days I managed to save enough bread for the toast and our men were treated to their much favored toast. Yes, our sugar issue came through on time and I got back my gold certificate. This ten spot was my lucky piece. Though I never spent it while in France I did use it as collateral, even to borrow francs. There were so few of them floating around that it was like a rare coin. It would buy more francs than the more common silver certificates or bank notes.

Chapter 9

Our first stop on the way to the trenches placed us in a camp probably two miles or more from the German line, not very far south east of Verdun. We were within range of German artillery and in a territory that had seen heavy fighting in the early months of the war and a continuous pounding by the enemy artillery. At the time we were in the area, both sides were simply carrying on a hold the line policy, each shelling daily, cross roads, watering places and arteries for the movement of soldiers, each sending out occasional raiding parties, mainly to take prisoners and to test the strength of their respective enemy's lines, and, on our part, to give our troops training and experience.

The small towns in the area had been shelled so often that they were shambles of disorderly piled building stones with parts of some of their thicker walls still standing. These mutilated structures in the greyish light of a descending moon cast ghost-like shadows through the demolished village. Those nearest the front were so badly damaged that they were not used for housing of troops. However, a passage way through them was kept up for the movement of troops and supplies to and from the front-line trenches. In a few there were large cellars still in good condition and being further covered by debris from the destroyed house were an excellent protection from bomb or artillery shells. These furnished good quarters for a few men. In one particular case, I remember locating our field kitchen in one of these, and it fell to my lot one night in this village to guard the kitchen and the men's quarters. I remember this night in particular because in this case I used the stone wall's shadows so as to remain hidden from approaching men until I was able to identify them.

Also on this occasion, the fellows in the kitchen cellar started shooting off their rifles at large rats and immediately following their blazing away at the rats, the machine guns on the nearby line took up the clatter and then the one-pounders and light artillery just back of us took a hand and flares and star shells started sizzling into the sky. It was quite a show for a short time and had all the racket of a small war. So far as I was able to learn, the total casualty list resulting from the thousands of rounds of ammunition that cracked, barged and roared into the still, moonlit night was three dead rats.

70

Our move from our first camp came before the above incident. It placed our company in support of a French position with one of our company's platoons in the range of a German machine gun. While our people fight a war as if it will be over in a few months, the French do the thing as if it is a way of life. The site and development of our new camp carried out the idea that this camp is a lovely place to come and relax in comfort after a weary uncomfortable stay of a short time in the muddy trenches just over the hill.

The small size bunk houses like the one assigned to me were on a tiny flat dug in the steep hillside on the opposite side from which Germany artillery shells would be fired, making it practically impossible for a shell to land on one of them. The placed runways and walks had protected railings alongside the step inclines that would have done justice to an American park.

In contrast with our boys, who reminded one of prancing young colts just beginning to feel the strength of their approaching maturity, the old French soldat brought to my mind images of a fireside and peaceful puffs from a corncob pipe, and, specifically, an uncle of mine, a veteran of the Spanish-American War who was a quiet, tall, lank, good natured soldier. The only French sight I saw that brought images of glamour, the sound of drum rolls and echoes of long past glories, was while the Rheims-Soissons drive was plowing its way to an end.

I was standing on a small knoll looking down a wide sunken road and out into a hidden court yard, when from their hideout behind a stone wall came dashing a French cavalry troop dressed in their shining parade garb, and up the road they came, and out of its mouth at the top of the grade without pausing or slacking their speed, they spread out in a skirmish line and went dashing across an open field and over the hill's crest dropping from my sight, with all the grace and speed of a racetrack prima donna.

Every new place has its own sense of greetings, some are rather harsh and are as uninviting as the growl of an angry dog. But this camp had a sense of welcome that made one feel as welcome as does a wide-bottom rocking chair. I was delighted at what I saw there. One glance around and about was enough, and I was in love with the place. The lovely trees hid us from the hungry eyes of any German

71

flying bomber that might be wandering around upstairs hunting for a target.

A quick inspection of my assigned hut and bunk put me on the jump to make a good thing better. I had found that my bunk consisted of poultry wire stretched between two-by-fours attached to four posts. By a combination of imagination, ingenuity and stealth, two Irish potato sacks obtained at the ration dump became a bunk mattress and for me at that time a comfortable bed.

Before this I had never been in a front line trench or seen men lined up facing each other waiting to kill, and was in too big a hurry to wait being sent into the lines. So I resolved to visit our company's platoon that was in close support position, and possibly the front line which was occupied by French soldiers. To do this was very unmilitary and seldom attempted by a private without orders. Each man had his place and had better not be caught out of it.

Anyway, one day I went on an exploration trip through this platoon's section. Before arriving at the platoon's station, I discovered near the traveling route I had taken an old, washed-out trench at the bottom of which was a path of sorts that indicated that soldiers passed that way often. Curiosity took over and caution for the time was laid aside. I made my way slowly down the old trench. Pretty soon I came to a sandbagged, camouflaged enclosure with an entrance just large enough for one to crawl through, which I did.

I had landed inside a genuine, well made and long kept, advance machine gun post. This post was manned by two old timers of the French army. They seemed glad to see me. It was all quiet along the whole front and my visit was a break in the long wait for something to happen in a lonely post. From the look-out hole left open for the purpose of spying unseen on the enemy, I got a good bird's eye view of the German line and on beyond to the extent of my seeing ability. Through the observation slot, I could actually see Germans moving around over there on their side. I could speak very little unreadable French but did manage to ask them why they did not fire on the Germans. Their answer came back to the effect that if they started shooting so would the Germans.

While new to the fighting business, we Americans thought that was a strange way to carry on a fighting war, but in time we

Americans learned that there were times when these unspoken truces were practical and appreciated by us as much as by the French. Like football, boxing, or any other game or contest, there must be rest periods, regrouping, replacements and a new preparation for big and little battles in the game of war.

The two old soldiers seemed to be amused and excited about something that had happened the night before. I could not make head or tail of what they were trying to tell me. They flapped their arms as if trying to imitate something flying, they barked like dogs and pantomimed little devils. It was confusing and, of course, aroused my curiosity. It seemed to me somehow related to the Marine platoon that was located just about them on the ridge. One of the statements I understood for sure and remember was, "The Marine officer is a bon soldat."

I didn't have much time to spare and cut my visit short, said good-bye to the old friendly soldiers and crawled back through the entrance hole and made my way back to the woods at the top of the hill. There I ran across a friend of mine who showed me his lieutenant's dugout and the holes in the dugout door where German machine bullets had gone through. These holes were a badge of honor to the soldier; it proved that they had been under enemy fire.

The men had been up the greater part of the night before, and practically all of them were in their grave-like foxholes, asleep. My friend was full of news and running over with talk. Now, with the information I received from him, I could interpret the talk and pantomime of the old French soldiers.

First, a reminder that enlisted men do not have bedrolls to sleep in. In this case and more often than not, there were no available dugouts for the enlisted men in the support area of the front lines. The enlisted men lay down to sleep fully dressed with shoes on, their gas masks within arm's length, their helmets under their heads serving as a pillow and their rifles at their side.

The lieutenant had a nice dry dugout with bunk and private sleeping bag, the envy of all who had none. He had no earthly reason to suspect that there would be an attack that night and the devil was present to urge him on. "So why not," the lieutenant reasoned, "a bath and a nice clean night shirt?" Then further protected from the chilly night by his sleeping bag, he was all set for a beautiful, comfortable sleep, a luxury that fighting, men often crave and sometimes have an opportunity to enjoy. All for a time was quiet and serene, not a single flare had gone sizzling into the sky, not a crack of a fired rifle had been heard, and machine gunners seemed to be taking a night off. A silent night it was, a restful one and the kind that encourages pleasant dreams, but it wouldn't last for this was the devil's night and he had planned to trap the good lieutenant. All hell broke loose. Light flares and signal rockets hissed and sputted their way into the blue sky. The crack of rifles punctured the silence followed by the clatter and roar of many heavy machine guns. Whiz-bangs of the close-ranged artillery shells flashed and the earth trembled with vibration as the big boys found their way to earth and their target.

Within seconds of the first roar and the crack of a rifle, the enlisted men bounced to their booted feet, pulled their helmet strap to its place under their chin, adjusted their gas masks, swooped up their rifles and were on their way to assemble in front of the lieutenant's dugout. The poor lieutenant, in that pitch-dark pit, dressed only in a nightshirt, what can he do? He met the test, that's what! With his nightshirt tail following behind, he came dashing out of his dugout with his gat in one hand and his boots in the other, snapped an order and somehow wangled his sockless feet into his boots and yelled, "Follow me."

It was already planned and rearranged where they would go in case of an attack. There were no pause or hesitation, they literally flew down that hill to an empty trench that was ready to receive them and from which the fire from their rifles and automatic rifle fire joined that of the French soldiers scattered along that sector of the front. The light from numerous rockets had given a weird, ghostly-appearing scene to the hillside that, when added to the ghost-like figures floating through the air looked like a pack of demon dogs. According to the Frenchman's pantomimes, it scared the daylights out of the Germans and sent them scooting back to their home trenches. Whether it was their ghostly and demon-like arrival or the speed of reinforcement, it doesn't matter, for our side won and in the words of the old Frenchman, and in terms we common soldiers understood, the lieutenant was a "bon soldat.".

Those men who followed their leader that night respected and loved their lieutenant. They admired him for the way he performed under a most critical chain of circumstances, that proved him to be the type of person that in times of crisis forgot his own dignity and personal welfare and threw himself enthusiastically into the task at hand. On that occasion speed was the key to success and that's what it got from him. If a force of Germans had beat him to his designated trench it could have been bad, very bad for him and his men. His men acted as brave soldiers should and gloried in their own spunk. They were unanimous in praise of their leader, but boy-like just couldn't help snickering a wee bit as they followed his shirt tail back to camp in the approaching light of an early morning.

We are again on the move, this time my company will take over a whole section of the front line trenches. We are to relieve another outfit of Marines. To reach our section on the front, we have to approach it by way of a hillside communication trench that has been there for years. It is more like a wide, deep, hillside gully than a man-made trench. Its bottom oozes with mud and contains almost knee-deep pot holes filled with churned-up mud and water. The banks are seeping wet from winter thaws and early spring rains. Though the days are warm and balmy, the nights are chilly and it will be days and maybe longer before the trenches are dry and comfortable. It was through this stirred-up slush we splashed our way to our fighting trench.

The trench my company took over was about seven and one-half feet deep on the side facing the German line and on the back side probably close to six and one-half feet deep. On the side facing the front there was a step-up firing stand that enabled one to stand and see across No-Man's Land that separated the two fronts. At the time we arrived to relieve and take over in place of the company that was there, they were lined up along the firing stand blasting away with all their power toward the German lines. I jumped up on the firing stand and took a look. It was dark out there in No-Man's Land. I didn't see anything to shoot at and turned to one of their fellows near me and asked him, "What are you shooting at?" His reply was, "The flash of their guns." I didn't see any flashes but did see lightning-like blinks and interpreted those blinks to be my target and

75

joined in the shooting. About the third man down the line from me was one of our platoon's automatic riflemen. He in his enthusiasm to get at the Germans had crawled out on top of the parapet and was lying there exposed to the enemy fire. When our lieutenant came up and saw the position he was in, there being too much noise for the lieutenant to be heard, he reached up and caught the gunner by his ankle and dragged him back into the protection of the trench. For some unknown reason there were no lights or signal rockets being shot into the air between the two forces as was the usual procedure when the two sides started shooting at each other at night.

The shooting did not continue very long after we arrived. In a short time we could not see any targets to shoot at or other indications that the Germans were out there in No-Man's Land. Indeed, I am inclined to suspect the bunch to be relieved started the shooting as a sort of show for us to walk into. Such action was highly unmilitary and out of order. Anyway they soon left and we took charge of the trenches. My platoon occupied only a very small part of a large sector occupied by our division and I know nothing of what was taking place on the line any distance from us. However, the next morning I learned that a sergeant in my company was killed during the shooting. As to details of his death I have none to give. Other than the death of the sergeant, in the eyes of most people there was nothing to report worthy of recording in our little shooting fray. However, to me it was very significant that these men who had not previously had an opportunity to shoot at the enemy did without orders or any apparent fear for their own safety, just crawl upon the firing line and in a businesslike manner began taking a part in the battle. The action of both the lieutenant and the gunner was commendable. It was dark and we could not see for ourselves and for all we know there could have been hundreds of Germans approaching and charging the trench.

Chapter 10

It was early spring, the surplus water left there by winter snow, ice and rain had not drained away. Our communicating trench that connected the front line trenches with the woods back in our rear was full of mud holes and the water was still seeping from its sides. The nights were very chilly and the damp cold earth made our dugout uncomfortable, except when heated by the small wood-burning stove left there by the French. The scenery in all directions bore the ugly scars of three and one-half years of war. We were in the fighting area made famous by the Battle of Verdun, but which was at this time a quiet sector and was used as an advance training area for American troops. It was here that we got our first baptism of fire and proved to ourselves, if not to the doubting French, worthy to be trusted with more dangerous and more important fronts and fighting assignments.

Out in front of us was No Man's Land with row after row of barbed-wire entanglements. Here and there were a few apple trees. A few wild flowers had begun to push up through the spring soil, bringing back pleasant memories of other days and pleasant dreams of the past. As I took special note of some violets that had begun to pop into view, I remembered having known girls to press violets between book pages and save them as a keepsake. With this thought came an inspiration.. "How nice it would be to send my friend back home a bouquet of violets gathered from No Man's Land." My mind made a quick trip to Georgia and I could see the little teacher girlfriend of mine letting the fourth-graders admire those violets that came all the way from a battle front in France. Then I formulated this plan of action. I would write two letters. In one I would place a bunch of violets and in it say nothing of flowers. In the other, I would suggest that after the war was over for her to come to France and how nice it would be to ramble over the old No Man's Lands together, and pick flowers from the forbidden land. Thus two letters written in the same day were all the clues she would need to get the message that the violets were from No Man's Land.

I caught a time when everything on the front was quiet and peaceful on the front and our lieutenant was back in his dugout asleep. I crawled out into No Man's Land and through the barbed wire and making myself as inconspicuous as possible made my way to a thick patch of violets, quickly picked a nice small bunch and hurried back into the trenches without mishap. Then I placed the violets in a letter and gave it to a friend who was going back to headquarters and requested him to have the chaplain censor and mail it for me. The other letter was turned over to the lieutenant to censor and have mailed for me.

My little friend teacher got the two letters, the fourth-graders saw and were given the privilege of touching flowers grown in No Man's Land and I had the joy of getting by the censors. I did other things and got by with some things that our local paper editor censored before publishing a letter of mine.

The trench was our home. For sanitary reasons we made use of an open air latrine just back of our trench. This place was under the observation of a German rifleman and once in a long while he would send a bullet into it, putting anyone who happened to be there at the time on the jump. I really don't think he was really trying to kill, but more likely doing the shooting for the fun of it and just to see the fellow scurry around in a hop-skip, an embarrassing as well as comical move to escape being hit.

We were out of wood for our dugout stove and I had volunteered to do something about it. Looking the ground over from the top of our trench, I spotted some dead limbs around an apple tree not very far from the trench and didn't think it too big a risk to go after them. There were plenty of times that we just didn't bother to shoot at a soldier at the distance that separated the two lines and, like the old Frenchman said, both sides were willing most of the time to leave off the shooting, especially when it was obvious that the fellow was on a friendly mission. While both sides seemed to be in the mood for peace, I decided it a proper time to venture out. Barbed wire is a mess to tangle with but one may maneuver his way around and through the most favorable passage ways without getting stuck or badly scratched.

I had made it through without too much trouble and was busy picking up dead twigs from the ground, when I happened to glance up in the direction of the German line and saw flying rather low and coming toward me a German plane. Like a chicken when a hawk is around, there was just one thing to do when an enemy plane comes in your direction – get under cover. The only cover in a jump-dive distance was an apple tree, and under it I landed pretty much as one goes into second base on a forced run. It was entirely possible that I had not been seen and that the plane would go on some place else and leave me alone. But not this time. That guy fired a burst from his machine gun and passed harmlessly on. Now what was that for? Was he trying to shoot me, or was that a signal for his artillery fire? Well, I would mighty quick find out. In the meantime, the fellows in the trench had taken note of what was happening and were lining up to watch the fun. You may think it fun to watch an old-time sack race but you haven't seen anything until you have seen a soldier outrun artillery fire with barbed wire entanglements as a handicap.

As was suspected, the machine gun shots were a signal to his artillery. The first shell clipped the top out of the apple tree under which I was hiding, and it took me only seconds to figure that the tree was the range marker for the artillery fire and believe you me, I shot out from under that tree like a bat out of the fiery furnace and was on my way headed for my trench. The chances are greater than ten to one that a man upright on his feet will be hit by an exploding shell than if he is lying flat on the ground. So one in my predicament will up and start running a few seconds after the shell explodes, very soon he will hear another one coming, and he will again dive to the ground and when it explodes jump up and start running again. This diving to the ground and up running was repeated four or five times before I was able to make it through the wire into the safety of my trench. All the time it was going on, my buddies were yelling at me in the same spirit as they would have if it had been a sack race and I their runner. No question about it, they enjoyed the race. It was fun. I was their runner. They shouted instructions, they cursed and groaned when it occurred to them that I was slow or about to fail them. But all the same, their yells and cheers spurred me along, just as it would have in a base run for a needed score. Running, jumping, crawling, diving through holes in the wire barricade, called for timing and maneuvers ordinarily one does not possess. How I made it without getting a scratch comes close to being a miracle. I was too busy to have time to be scared and the shouts of my audience helped a lot.

The above episode was my first time to come close to meeting my death from falling shells. My escape from injury boosted my self-confidence and strengthened my faith in my own survival. It also taught me that vigorous activity with the mind concentrated on the problem of escape was a sure antidote to fear. It was good training of both the body and mind. I was practicing for a lot of other times when only doing the right thing stood between me and death. The episode furnished an intervention in the closed-in monotony of our daily routine and, of course, helped quicken my reflex muscular actions when under shell fire.

Now a pole carried by two men loaded to feed and furnish coffee for a large number of men, all hungry and with healthy appetites, is no child's play under any circumstances, and when it has to be carried down a water-clogged, sticky, mud hole route it becomes a really painful task. Even so, two trips per days and part of the time three back of the line and the extras one picks up at the kitchen is very rewarding, not to mention the opportunity of a bath, a change of clothes and the soothing feeling to tired, dirty feet to sit and let cold spring water soak away the burn and itch caused by having gone too long without washing the feet and a change of socks. After forty odd years, one's memory does not register time accurately and I would not swear to a lot of statements in this manuscript. I know it seemed like a long, long time and believe it was close to twenty days that we stayed in those trenches and equally that long before these men had a real bath and probably that long before some had removed their clothes before lying down to sleep. I am telling you these things that you may know that the little common things about a soldier's life when added up become very big and that I am not kidding when I tell you that it is very rewarding to be able to change one's socks and just sit and let nice cool water run over tired burning feet. So, I was happy to be on the chow detail and now you know why.

Yet, that mud, the sticky mud, I hated it. I despised it. How to hold on to my chow job and at the same time avoid those trips through the mud was my problem. Thus you will understand it was not that I was especially brave, or that I was a sort of daring somebody, but fear of the German sharpshooters or shells that led me to take risks and expose myself to the enemy fire. Furthermore, I figured I could outsmart them and their mechanical, routine way of doing things. I had been taught to obey orders and leave the thinking to our superiors. While I prescribed to that theory in principle myself and never went directly contrary to a specific order directed at me, I do know that each individual has little problems that only he understands and only he can solve.

Anyway, that noon when we reached the place in the woods where the communication trench started, I turned from the path that led into the trench and took a course close to and parallel to it. My partner started to argue about the danger of exposing ourselves to the eyes of the Germans. I assured him that the Germans were not expecting us to show ourselves and that before they saw us and had time to figure the range and have their artillery gun trained on us we would be safe in our trench. It worked as I thought it would, and we were not fired on.

That night I led my partner into the trench and down it. My partner glared at me and said, "Hemrick, I just can't understand you; in daytime you go down that hillside, wide open trail exposing us to the Germans."

"Certainly," was my reply. "You must surely have noticed that the Germans get the range on spots in the day time, but do most of their shelling at night, because that is when most soldiers are on the move and, like you, are not afraid of being seen. They could just for the hell of it start shelling this side of the hill tonight, then where would we be? At night, we cannot see the pattern of their fire and cannot see well enough to run without falling down and losing the chow. So, we stay in the trench on our night trips and play it safe."

The next day when we left the kitchen, I took a right hand turn, a direction which placed us in the woods on the opposite side of the hill from where we went down the day before. When we arrived at the edge of the woods, we halted a few minutes before going out in the open. It was my contention that the Germans had us timed and that they would be expecting us to return with the chow for our men about the same time following the same route as we took the day before and would certainly be delighted for an opportunity to ruin our men's chow.

A German artilleryman was waiting with his gun trained on yesterday's route. Our men in the trenches had it figured the same way. They were lined up down there in their trench watching the route and wondering why in the hell we didn't come on with their chow. We two chow hands had shouldered the chow pole and were all set to go. Our wait was over. The Germans had turned loose their first shells, and true to expectations, dropped them in the tracks we had made the day before. The chow hands knowing now that they had guessed right, took a fast trot down the hill. At the explosion of the first shell, as you would imagine, curses and groans growled from the throats of the men in trench for they, like the Germans, were expecting us to return the route the shells were landing on. Then some guy spotted us coming down the other side of the hill and the cry went roaring up the hill, "THERE THEY COME!" And the groans became shouts of joy. The curses changed to cheers and praise and we were made to feel like heroes who had out-smarted the Great Kaiser and saved their chow.

This true episode had all the elements and thrills of a great victory, either of a war battle or a peace-time contest between opposing teams and our side won. The idea of total war is a curse on humanity, invented and developed by self-righteous civilians under the supervision of the devil.

It is another day and time for another chow run, or shall we take the safe route and go slogging through the mud? Well, I don't know, it could be that we have gotten the Germans' dander up and they may feel it a point of honor that they teach those rocky chow hands a lesson. But the mud, darn the mud, darn the Germans, we will play it by ear. We will head half-way between the two ends of the hillside and be prepared to shift to any one of the three routes down the hill. We would be stopping at the edge of the woods for rest and meditation on which route to take, and after looking the situation over if we considered it too dangerous to go openly down the hill we would go through the woods to the communication trench and down it.

As we made our way through the woods, we could hear shells as they exploded and realized that the Germans had already begun dropping shells on our hill route. But we kept going on our chosen middle route through the woods. As we drew near the edge of the woods at the top of the hill the shelling stopped. Near the point where we stopped was a heavy machine gun position and on reaching the place one of the gunners came out and warned us against taking that route to our trench. He told us that the German artillery had been shelling the whole hillside. The idea came to me that the German artillerymen didn't give a hoot whether they hit us or not, that they had been ordered to drop fifteen or twenty shells on the hillside and having carried out that order were no longer interested in the hill and probably getting ready to eat their own chow and it was safer now than if they had not just finished shelling it. On the other hand, some guy back there might figure that's the way I would figure it and save one of his guns back in reserve to be ready for action if that proved to be the case. The boys in the trench had been on the lookout for their chow since the first shell had fallen in that area. They had forgotten about the thrill and fun they had enjoyed the day before. All they could think about now was their chow and were ready to abuse us for taking unnecessary risks with it. They were in no mood to enjoy another close race with their chow at stake. If we failed them it would be a long wait for another meal and their empty stomachs were already growling for attention. My reputation was O.K., but their concern was of today and not yesterday or any other days gone by.

They were lined up inside their trench and were searching the whole hillside for some sign of us. No doubt they were making us the butt of various sarcastic remarks and curses in mule skinner's language as well as in Marine lingo! Otherwise, everything was quiet and peaceful all along the front. There were no visible evidence of war near our sector. Nevertheless, we two chow hands made ready for a record dash run. We didn't really expect much trouble, but by gosh, we didn't choose to make it easy for anyone who might try to get us. I don't know the record for a two-hundred yard dash, but whatever it is, with exploding shells falling just back of our heels you can imagine we picked them up and let them down with a speed that no ordinary track runner could beat. At least one German gun crew and its fire spotter had begun to catch on to the crazy idea that one chow hand had that he could out-smart the German army. The gun crew was ready and standing by. The spotter was ready to call the shots, and then the fast moving target, the two chow hands, had come out of the woods. With the mechanical smoothness of years of practice, the spotter gave his orders. With equal positive movements the proper adjustments were made and a shell was on its journey to fall just at our backs, followed by another to fall where we had been a few seconds ago. But we were moving fast now and as the gunners dropped their shells farther down the hill, we increased our speed to a dead run. This was bad. This was serious. Could we outrun the planned fire pattern of the gun crew? No fooling there. It sparked of grim determination and the use of scientific calculation of the time it took for two chow hands to travel two hundred yards with a load of chow. As we moved farther down the hill so did the falling shells always just a few yards back of us. Would they catch and pass us as it was planned to do? Maybe not! For we were not heavy-booted solders of the Fatherland and their scientific calculations were based on sluggish, loose-booted German foot soldiers. We were, for at least this race, scared fleet Americans much faster than any average chow runners. Spurred on by those shells dropping just back of our heels the pendulum swing of our legs grew faster and faster and with each new falling and exploding shell. The length between the rise and landing of our feet was widening to unusual lengths. We outran the spotter's calculations and with, the aid of our downhill pull and my luck we landed in our trench just seconds and a couple of jumps before his shell pattern could catch up with us. Seconds made the difference. Hallelujah. We won another victory over the Kaiser!

There were no cheers or shouted instructions from the fellows in the trenches this time. Their hearts had risen dangerously high in their throats. They were for once frightened into silence. Their chow appeared hopelessly lost to them. The danger was too great and the situation too serious for words. It was like having a razor blade at their throats. They could hardly breathe. Their nervous tension froze their emotions into hopelessness and people just don't shout and carry on when they are faced with a hopeless situation. With the chow safe in the trench, with their Adam's apples back in place, and their stomachs back near normal, the enforced quiet of the sputtering, angry men exploded with an outburst of curses. They quickly told the two chow-hands off for foolishly exposing their chow to shell fire. There was no formally held kangaroo court, none was needed. The men were unanimous and the verdict was, "If you two guys again expose our chow on that hill, if the Germans don't get you, we will." The men were in no mood to argue the ,case and I knew it, and what's more, believe me, I had had the daylights scared out of me. The same went for my partner and we were happy to have it appear that we hereafter would play it safe because they had so ordered it.

The fighting we had done was more like a pre-season contest between two friendly rival football squads than a mid-season battle to save the honor of one's alma mater. More like friendly rivals training with live ammunition than angry enemies in a fight to kill each other. It was like giving a fellow a chance to learn his trade and how bad it could be, without killing him. Next, and soon to come, was the big game, a fight unto death.

The German Army was on the rampant, winning victory after victory and making a desperate effort to destroy the Allied forces and bring a quick end to the war.

Chapter 11

World War I had reached its last and final stage it would stagger along for a while longer, but neither the Germans, French or English could survive much longer the evil effects of the war. The battles of the coming months would decide the fate of the German nation and the part our soldiers would play in the late and last stages of the war, as well as President Wilson's part in drawing up the peace treaty. We soldiers knew that we would be filling a major role in these coming events, but when and where, that was the problem that was bothering our battalion's colonel and high ranking officers all the way up to Marshal Foch.

In the game of war as in the game of football, the opposing team may upset the offensive plans of the enemy by a drive of their own, and that is what happened in May 1918. The Germans jumped the gun on our forces and started their drive before we were ready. The Germans knew the war was approaching its end and had reasoned that it was now or never, too many Americans were getting ready to enter the fight. England and especially France were so weakened that a real knock-out blow now could very well end the war in their favor. They put their all in one grand effort with the English-held seaports on the North Sea and the city of Paris as their goals.

The Germans were so successful in their drive, so many French soldiers and so much of their equipment was lost, that many of their tired, worn-out remaining soldiers lost the will to fight. Their retreat was fast and their losses great, and the Germans were advancing toward Paris about as fast as an army of men and mules could travel. The remaining, thin French lines that stood between the Germans and their prized goal, Paris, were almost in a panic and the morale of the French soldiers and people was in very bad shape, for at the rate the enemy was advancing, they would be in a matter of days in shelling range of Paris. And the French people would be greatly tempted to surrender and sue for peace. All of which made it necessary for an all-over change of plans for a drive of their own.

Ours was a restless outfit. The eternal urge to move was with us again. The mud stains gathered in the trenches had practically faded from our uniforms, and the dust and sweat-grime accumulated during our hike to our present village had been scrubbed from our skin and clothes. Our equipment had been repaired and replaced where needed, our shoes cleaned, our hair cut and our faces were adjusted to a clean shave. From active memory was gone to near forgetfulness the misery of the other places. "What's just around the next corner? Let's go see." Such was our mood when the orders came to pack and get in readiness for another move.

We had traveled by way of small French trains and learned to love the lonesome wail of the miniature locomotives as they rolled along the countryside. We had watched with open-eyed wonder and interest from our place in the freight yards as the Frenchmen moved the cars here and there with the aid of animal horse power. We had learned to expect and know that, if we had time to spare, our feet and legs were our official means of transportation from place to place. We often had the pleasant surprise of seeing something new and different while traveling around. New faces, new scenes and new experiences and something different was what we craved. Even a red-headed baby, called Souvenir, resting in the arms of a dark woman aroused our curiosity and speculation as to its daddy. The baby was a gift from some red-headed Yankee soldier. Well, don't let it shock you to learn that our gifts included red-headed and black babies along with cigarettes and candy bars.

We were on our way marching in the usual way, all set for a long, free-swinging leg hike when halted and allowed to "fall-out" of ranks alongside a village street. Then there came drifting down to us, followed by a husky spontaneous cheer, the information that we would be carried to our destination in trucks. Now, a ride, any kind of a ride, was very exceptional, and something to excite our curiosity. But that was not all.

"Wow, what's this?"

"Oh boy, don't we rate!"

"A between-meal sandwich !"

"Next thing you know they will be giving us limousines to ride in, along with afternoon tea."

These and a lot of other remarks brought on by the truck ride announcement and the appearance of fat meat sandwiches were brought to a sudden hush by another announcement, that the sandwich each man received was the last meal he would get that day. Then it suddenly occurred to me that while we were being carried along by gasoline power at a rapid rate, our kitchen and supplies would be trailing along, pulled by lazy mules.

After hours of delay, our impatient wait came to an end and the men sprang to their feet and shouted a jubilant welcome as fifty odd trucks driven by Chinese drivers lined up alongside of the men of the Second Battalion of the Sixth Regiment of Marines. They were big, powerful motor trucks, French machines, with plank seats and canvas covered tops. Each truck was loaded with approximately twenty men with their sixty pound packs, rifles and other fighting equipment. Some of the other battalions of the Sixth had gone on before and others would follow. The Second Division was ready and willing, available and anxious to demonstrate its ability to fight. A lone Third Division machine gun battalion was rushed on ahead to join a French force and together prevent the Germans from crossing the river bridge at Chateau-Thiery.

A mighty army of Germans like the sweeping destructive force of a flooded river had broken the French lines that guarded the gateway to Paris, overflowed the country and were sweeping aside all the remaining resistance left in its path.

The French commander-in-chief dared not weaken his lines on other fronts. He could not take the risk of demoralizing all his troops by weakening the lines of the whole front by a big shift of his forces to the Chateau-Thiery area. The French command was stumped, frustrated, and couldn't decide which way to move. The American Second Army Division was available, and yet the French authorities hesitated to order it there, to close the gate that blocked the road to Paris. There was doubt in their minds that a green American division could stop the Germans. So in the end they put off making a final decision. Instead, they ordered the division to proceed to Meau and wait there for further orders. In the meantime, while we were on our way to Meau, the Germans were advancing rapidly, and the French soldiers opposing them were losing their ability and will to take a stand and stop the drive on Paris. The situation continued to grow worse and had by the time we reached Meau become desperate. The indecision on the part of the French authorities, who were responsible for directing our division, gave orders and counter-orders and changes of plan for us that caused delay, confusion and hardships for our men. The colonel of our battalion, in the confusion of changing orders, was lost from his command and wandered around for most of the night of May 31st looking for us. As I look back and try to untangle the mix-up situation we were in on that night and several days to follow, it appears exceedingly difficult, and comes close to being a miracle that two dozen or more separate military convoys of small and large units of military forces traveling different routes in a strange country, handicapped by a language barrier, indecisions and changing of orders could and did assemble and form a united front line in the face of an advancing strong enemy, all in the course of a couple of days.

The rank and file of the enlisted men who boarded those trucks had not been reading any newspapers, seen any official war reports or contacted anyone who had. We had no reason to suspect that a large number of us were making our last move.

The people who lived in the towns and villages through which we passed did know. They had read the news and had talked with the first of the fleeing refugees who had possessed personal means of fast transportation that had brought them from near the disastrous fighting front.

Early in our journey, the natives had lined the streets in surprising large numbers and waved us on. Our fellows were jubilant in spirit and showed it by song, shouts and laughter. Why shouldn't we be happy? We were moving to new adventures and these people had left their plows, their shops and household duties to honor us. The passing of fifty odd truck loads of foreign soldiers was not a strange, inexperienced sight to these people, who had lived through three years of war. We on the face of it evidently were something special; we were being given a recognition usually reserved for distinguished parties, such as a president, famous generals and war heroes. (That's what we thought.)

These people appeared to be excited and pleased to see us and the long line of trucks loaded with soldiers go by. Yet I got the impression that there was something wrong with the spirit that was predominant in the crowds. There was an apparent mixture of sadness, fear and pleasure registered on their different faces. It just wasn't natural, the opposite and conflicting emotions shown and displayed by the crowds of French people who had come out merrily to see a parade of soldiers go by. They were not, in any sense of the word, jubilant and their feelings as expressed by their faces did not justify the assumption that they had turned out to honor us as they would have a distinguished personage passing through their village. They left me puzzled and I began to ponder about what had come over them.

Now that I know the situation as it existed at that time, I can venture an interpretation of what I saw. They were terribly frightened with the fear that the Germans would reach their town, saddened by the loss of many friends and relatives in the recent battles, pleased to see aid going forward to stop the enemy and also puzzled to know what manner of men were these Americans who in the face of such a crisis could be in such a joyful spirit. They probably had a mixture of doubt of our sanity, with an admiration for our courage, as we seemingly were happily and joyfully hurrying to our venture with defeat and death. There was some hope, not much, for how could we inexperienced fighters succeed where their own soldiers had failed?

There were those, a few no doubt, who believed that they were experiencing a historical event similar to another one that had happened years before and that this one, too, would fill many pages of French history, and that they were to be eyewitness to history in the making. Some of them had lived through another crisis when soldiers were rushing by to turn the tidal wave of another advancing thrust directed at their beloved Paris. All those present, including school children, knew from the tales of their elders, that soldiers on bicycles, in horse-drawn taxi cabs from Paris, walking, and by all other available means of travel, had passed through their village on the same mission as ours – to fight back a German army that at that distant time had broken through their defense and was advancing on Paris. History was repeating itself.

The crowds had gathered along the Metz-Paris road not to honor us because of the things we had done in the past, but for what we might be able to do in the future and because they knew if help reached their soldiers in time to save their towns it would have to

90

come the route we were following. It is possible that they had heard rumors that Americans were coming and wanted to see what manner of soldiers we were. They would have been happier and more enthusiastic with their cheers if instead of us, the trucks had carried their own famous fighting units such as the French Blue Devils, or even Scottish Ladies from Hell. Of course we were welcome, any soldiers would have been, and cheered on with a wish and a prayer.

Our caravan passed Paris a few miles north of the city. Even in normal times the road along this route would have been jammed with traffic. At the time we made the journey it was much worse than normal. There were increasing movements of both soldiers and military supplies as well as civilians. The fact that most of these people were tired, worn-out and drowsy from loss of sleep increased the road hazards. There were many wrecks that slowed, delayed and halted our progress. My memory of the trip registers an overall picture and specific incidents that I saw. The small incidents are like individual pieces of a put-together picture puzzle; they are scrambled in a way that does not make a continued flow in time or location.

As we moved along we noticed a gradual thickening of the traffic. More of it appeared to be southbound. In fact the only traffic we saw headed north was apparently on military business of some sort. The sides of the road were more crowded with people, but a change had taken place. These people were not there to see us go by; they were not local people; they were refugees fleeing from the German Army. They were on the side of the road because they were tired and exhausted from their many hours of struggle to escape from the advancing Germans. There were no smiles on their faces, no waving of their hands; instead their faces were pale and showed signs of fear and despair. All that could stayed on the move, only stopping when their tired limbs could no longer move along in the line of traffic.

On the side of the road were sick, wounded and deadly tired soldiers, old tottering men and women. Almost everyone of them were loaded down to and beyond their capacity to carry with their most precious possessions saved from their deserted homes. Some had their goods tied to the frames of old bicycles and were pushing them along. The more fortunate had their household goods loaded on two-wheel cars, most of them pulled by a horse, and some by manual labor. One old man was seen pushing a farm wheel barrow before him on which was sitting a feeble old lady. There were children, and some young mothers with babies in their arms, and others in a family way. Some of the children and babies were sick. One baby had died and its mother was beside the road weeping over the body of her lost child. There were dead horses and two-wheeled carts with both wheels smashed beyond repair. The remains of a wrecked, demolished truck was lying in a ditch near the road and a dilapidated wrecked touring car lay upside down.

The scene of human misery brought tears to the eyes and a silent prayer to the lips of godly men in the trucks and a curse filled with hate from the lips of the rogues. None were indifferent, none could be. What we saw was the product of war.

As we moved deeper into this stream of human misery our men for the first time were brought face to face with the fact that war was a sad business, a costly one whose product was mostly misery and despair, pain and death, a kind of reward only the devil and his kind could want or enjoy.

There were no more shouts or laughter coming from the men in our trucks. This was different. There was no jubilee for our men in this kind of war or fun to move along this kind of trail. Their mouths were set with grim sternness, their skin seemed to be drawn tightly over their high cheek bones, and their eyes did not sparkle with mischief any more. It was as if the emotional strain of witnessing so much misery had suddenly turned carefree youths into mature men. We rode along in silence. Thrills, adventure and glory did not show its face in this kind of war. Thus we moved along that part of the trail that was jammed with refugees. Our hearts and souls were captured by these people. This emotional experience was like a baptism of fire, a preparatory ritual, that qualified us for the task destiny had given us to perform. Pains of hunger, hurts from bullets and shells, tired muscles and lost sleep, all of these we would accept as our due and the emotional pay we would contribute to the people we saw along that trail of misery. The sum total of all of our woes could not match what we saw the refugees endure.

We had passed the end of the long line of refugees. It appeared that our caravan was alone on the road. Behind us was a moving mass of human miseries. In front of us was approaching a force whose aim was to kill and destroy. In between, where we were, calm and peaceful quiet dominated the scene. The refugees and wounded, and the remnants of the defeated, retreating French army were behind us; the dwindling lines of the bravest of the brave of the French forces still remained in front of us, to harass as best they could the advancing Germans. In our present area everything was still; nature had cooperated, and hardly a breeze was stirring. The empty fields, the traffic-less road and the deserted homes made ghostly the countryside where our caravan came to a stop and we, after hours upon hours sitting on uncushioned plank seats, made our way from the trucks into a wooded area beside the road to finish out the night bivouacked there. Our aching bodies dropped off into sound innocent slumber and an uninterrupted rest that lasted until the sun appeared over the hill and announced that another day had arrived.

As was and is usual with me, on the morning of June 1, 1918, wakefulness followed close behind the coming of daylight. With it the thought that we were isolated from the American supply lines and only time could tell when those slow moving mules that brought food supplies to us could travel that traffic-jammed trail that took some eighteen hours for our motor powered trucks to push through. Each man of us had with him a hunk of fatback, salt, pepper and some soda crackers, not exactly what a man wanted for breakfast. So I punched the guy next to me and whispered, "Follow me."

When a Frenchman leaves his home and takes to his heels in flight to escape capture by the Germans, he carries with him all his worldly goods possible. Each succeeding group of refugees and soldiers that pass that deserted home feels free to search the place for anything left that he needs or could use (In one case I remember sleeping on a feather bed some soldier brought into the trenches). When my buddy and I went out that early morning to find food to supplement the meager amount we carried in our packs we were in full knowledge of the prescribed customary practice that prevailed before the advance of the enemy's troops.

We knew that there wouldn't be much left in the deserted farm home that we had spotted nearby. But we believed in the theory that the early bird gets the worm, and acted accordingly. We quickly learned that the kitchen larder and cupboard were bare. Nothing eatable was found in the farm house. Next we searched the barn and found all the livestock and grain had been removed. But on further search back of the barn, near the trees, we found a lone hen scratching in the rich dirt. Perhaps she had escaped other food hunters by retreating into the underbrush where she could find a place to hide. We very carefully maneuvered her into the barnyard and with little trouble trapped and caught her. Then from the family's garden we gathered carrots and Irish potatoes. We didn't especially like raw carrots for breakfast but did eat a few of the most tender ones to sorter appease our stomachs until we could prepare our feast. Next we went back in the house to hunt and find a vessel in which to boil water for the scalding and cooking of our hen. From our packs we took coffee, salt and pepper. With these, plus crackers, the hen, potatoes and carrots, we began and prepared for ourselves a whopping big meal with some left over to go into our mess kit to be eaten later in the day.

It took time to do all this, but fortunately for us it took time for the commander of our brigade to contact us and to issue orders that would send us up the road to meet the retreating French and stop the German drive on Paris.

Thus it was that while the rest of our company were making a breakfast of poorly, individually cooked bacon, and crackers, my buddy and I, for breakfast, were stuffing ourselves on a farm-boy style hen mull with a side dish of boiled spuds and carrots. As I had estimated, it took some time for our government issue of food to catch up with us. The night of the second day, however, we did receive an issue of canned beef and crackers. It seemed that I had underestimated our brigade commander. It appears that he emptied some trucks carrying less-needed materials to other points, loaded them with supplies badly needed by the Marines, and rushed them to us. Anyway it was a solid month before this former chow hand got a chance to visit our company's rolling kitchen. I was back in the ranks pinned down to one small squad and there I would stay until the battles of Chateau-Thiery and Belleau Wood were won. While

I wasn't too good at killing Germans even our regimental band was used as stretcher bearers, and engineers were constantly alternating between fighting and doing regular engineers' work. As previously mentioned, our good old chaplain took a pick and shovel and helped in preparing a resting place for our dead.

The French in command of our forces did not think we could be ready to go into the line before the second of June. But the American officer in charge of the Second Division, General Harbord, thought different and was given permission to enter the lines the first day of June, 1918. At this point there was no visible, physical line. Such a line would be established where the two forces met. There we would dig in, stop and hold the Germans until we were ready to start a drive of our own, to destroy the German Army and end the war.

Our horse-drawn artillery was somewhere in the rear making their way to us with all speed possible by train and on foot. I can't be sure, but think it was more than two days before they were ready to give the infantry full support. Until their arrival the scattered, meager help given by the French artillery was poor. Some retreating French soldiers had lost contact with their command and would apparently just shell over in the direction they thought the Germans were coming.

I do not recall the time of day, but believe it was well in the forenoon of June the first that we were assembled by the side of the road ready to move on. As was often the case when we were preparing to move, someone in the line near me raised the question, "Where do we go from here?"

Our sergeant answered in these words: "For all we know we are on our way to hell."

The last news we had was in a note dropped by an airplane a short time ago which stated that the French forces were in full retreat and that the German soldiers were marching in squad formation down this road toward us. Our orders were to get into trucks, that would arrive there shortly, and go up the road until we met the retreating French soldiers, and we would then get out, form our lines, and there block the German drive on Paris.

In a matter of minutes the trucks arrived, we quickly boarded tem and were on our way. When we had reached our destination we left the trucks and from the road deployed in fighting formation and started taking a position that later became our temporary front. I could not see or know what was taking place over a six mile area but assume that the same procedure was to all practical purpose taking place all along the anticipated front of six miles. In one of the sectors the Germans came on and there was some immediate fighting. However, I didn't take part in any fighting for a few days.

I should state here that our source of information of German movements at that time was a plane that would fly up to the advancing Germans, take a look and fly back, not landing where we were but just drop a note and go on. I can't be sure about every platoon in my company but do know my part of it and I believe all of it was held in reserve in the early stage and I was not in the advance front line. My memory of the first night is very hazy but do I remember being on an ammunition detail and making one trip to the fighting line. We had established what might be called a fluid line, and until we had time to coordinate our different units, work out a system of communication, and become familiar with the territory over which we were operating, most of us would have a rather hazed, confused understanding of what was going on. Most of our movements were made at night, having no maps, no idea of the names of the places or of the geography of the area, I will have to limit myself to writing about the little incidents that occurred in the area occupied by me and forget about the other part of the front and the numerous small battles that were constantly being fought all along the six mile front.

Furthermore, I want you to keep in mind that I am writing from memory and without notes, so it is not to be expected that I can give the whole history of all the battles that took place in the area of Chateau-Thiery or remember all the engagements I took part in. Anyway, I believe it better to give samples of what happened to and near me. There was too much of it to give the whole story. It is also true that I cannot, at this late date, be accurate and keep the incidents in the order they occurred or at the place where they took place. Really, in my kind of story, accuracy in details is not required.

Chapter 12

The French were so sure that we would not be able to hold the lines we were establishing that, instead of stopping their retreat and joining us in the fight, they simply passed us by and went back several miles and started preparing a position for us to retreat to. The cocky enlisted Marines felt the danger but it made them angry for anyone to even hint that they might fail. The circumstances under which we moved into this dangerous position, which the French doubted that we would be able to hold, required bold quick action. Ammunition was the number one requirement for success. Contrary to the French idea of caution, Lucky, a town only a stone's throw from woods occupied by Germans at its nearest point, was made an ammunition dump for our section of the front and while I was there that first night a French soldier was complaining about so much ammunition and other supplies that close to the Germans and went so far as to say that the enemy would be there in possession of it and the whole town in no time. This made some of our fellows so angry that they cursed the Frenchman out and told him that we were Marines and "What's ours no damn German or anybody else could take it away from us."

The May 1918 breakthrough, the ease and rapidity of the German advance toward Paris was no doubt a pleasant surprise and a great boost to the morale of the German soldiers. The apparent demoralized flight and only scattered resistance of the French army brought back to the tired Germans those old goose-stepping pride and the emotional triumph of a conquering master race. The iron heel was again on the march and the captured French bread and wine added to their boosted spirits. So it was a happy, spirited, singing, victorious, proud German army – following on the heels of the retreating French – that came to a jolting halt as they came to and up against a new element and were confronted with a bunch of fresh, raw, but eager-to-fight American troops.

The Germans were professionals. They didn't expect or believe that the amateur, undisciplined, over-indulged, soft life our boys lived at home, plus absence of training and experience, could or would produce the physical toughness and the will to stand the pain and hardships required of a good fighting soldier. So the Germans waded into the Americans with the confidence of old time professionals expecting to smash and push them aside and get going on their march to Paris. To their surprise, these Americans did not push so easy. They were not weaklings, but were tough, rough and mean fighters whose ignorance of the fine points of the fighting profession was made up for by a crazy boldness that shocked and amazed the professionals.

Boldness, though costly, comes close to being a good substitute for knowledge in any kind of contest. One German officer is credited with accusing the Marines of being young devils recently released from hell. The professional's theory of the inherent weakness of a mushroom army is correct, but the Marines had been transformed and toughened up in a hardening off environment of hardships and torture.

The German drive was stopped; with the gateway to Paris closed, now what? The objectives and strategies of the two opposing forces became very similar in that each wanted to make his lines secure. But what was security for the one was in most cases insecurity for the other.

In several instances each wanted their lines to be located at the same place. This scramble for favorable positions was what the fighting was about that went on for almost six weeks in the area north west of Chateau-Thiery and in Belleau Wood.

The German effort, and ours, was like an aggressive football team's play to maneuver the line to a place in the battlefield where they could kick the ball, break through, or make an end run. Our plays were to first make our position secure, hold the Germans where they were, weakening and wearing them down while making ready for an end run miles from our present area. The time element was in our favor. The peak of German force and morale was on the decline, both the English and the French had used up their best forces in the long years of struggle. All three, France, England, Germany, could well be classed as tired and worn-out nations. There had been large pockets of mutiny in the French army and danger of more to follow. The Americans were an inexperienced and unfired relief, thrown into the line, not by choice, but in desperation for lack of other promising substitutes.

The Germans were in full awareness of the potential value and importance of the arrival of the Americans on the fighting front. Americans of the First Division had challenged the Germans in the area of Cantigny only a few days previous and now the Second Army Division was challenging them in the area of Chateau-Thiery and Belleau Wood. The success or failure of these two divisions was a determining factor for the rise or fall of the morale of the French and English soldiers, hence our success in these two engagements had a tremendous effect on the outlook of the war.

In carrying out our policy to shorten and make more secure our lines, and prevent the Germans from possessing the more favorable locations, we made dozens of small area attacks and advances that were costly in men and yet the sum total of all the little victories added up to the second battle of the Marne. Belleau Wood was a prized possession of the Germans because under the cover of this area they could assemble a massive amount of men and munitions of war for a breakthrough and a forward drive and do considerable damage to our forces. Therefore, this wooded area became the battlefield for some of the hardest and most deadly fighting the Marines had ever experienced.

Belleau Wood consisted of second growth trees so thick that in places one could see only a short distance through it. It also contained a lot of large rocks that in places furnished almost impregnable machine gun positions. Especially so, since in our attacks on them we didn't at times have needed rifle and hand grenades or mortar support and had to depend on rifle and automatic rifle fire to capture or kill the German gunners.

The Germans getting into the woods first had time to explore and make themselves familiar with the terrain, large rocks and boulders, ditches and other advantages that could be used for military purposes. We being ignorant of these things, the Germans had a great advantage in the fight over the area.

Trying to describe the fight over this piece of woods is like putting together a picture puzzle in the dark. There were times in the darkness of the night when one didn't know for sure where either his own people or the Germans were. The forward position of the two forces were so uncertain and so close together that artillery fire could not be safely used by either against the other's front line. The soldiers held in support caught it day and night, and often times suffered more losses than did the forces that were exchanging rifle and machine gun fire at the front. While I will be back with a few personal incidents that took place in the woods, for now let it suffice to say that our work was to drive the Germans out. The French government honored the Marines by naming this area The Marine Woods and the Germans were so impressed by our fighting that they gave us the title of Devil Dogs. This ranged the Marines along with the Blue Devils of France and The Ladies from Hell of Scotland. In the German's mind we were among the three top-ranking fighting units of World War I.

Fighting men, regardless of how they feel about Germans in other respects, are flattered to have themselves pointed out by the Germans as having fought like hell. We fought the Germans' best and won. Those fellows thought that only the devil could outfight them.

People just don't ignore the Marines. The reaction toward them is not always friendly. They are too cocky for some folks, and there are times when there is jealousy to be considered. They have some nicknames that aren't exactly complimentary, one of which is Bell Hops. During part of the time of World War I they received so much publicity that in some places the yell, "Who won the war? The Marines, the Marines," was sarcastically blared out.

The Ninth and Twenty-third Army Regiments were also a part of the Second Army Division and certainly contributed their part toward making it rank A-1 in France. The First Army Division's record was so darn close to our record that they too sometimes claim to equal the Second's record in France. But I am supposed to be writing about the Marines, the Devil Dogs and myself and not the whole army. May I say, it's up to you guys to toot your own horn.

The Marines hit the publicity jackpot at just the right time. The morale of the French soldiers was at an all-time low, in fact almost gone. The position of the English soldiers on their front was very shaky and the English command was crying for more American help. This call for help and our ability to give it was being watched around the world and the watchers were wondering about the quality of the quickly gathered together soldiers, at that time called Ninety Day Wonders, that were crowded into ships and sailed to France.

The many tales told of the Marines were shots in the arm, a badly needed stimulant for the weak hearts, not only of the French army, but also in the English and American, not to mention the adverse effect it would have on the German people. The Marines furnished a much needed victory.

We were not quitters, we would die before we would move out of those woods. They were ours, we had paid for them. More of our company's men were answering the Roll Call Up Yonder and lying in hospital beds than were left fighting in the woods. The lucky ones were wounded. The remainder of us were resolved that no Germans would take what's ours from us. We were covered with body lice, hungry and thirsty. We were bruised in body and soul, tired and weary, dirty and weakened by dysentery, that lousy messy kind that requires lots of paper and sanitation, but we had none. There was human blood on our hands that had to go for many days before they could be washed. We used that bacteria-filled, germ culture wood soil as our substitute for soap and water. Like Job, of old, we were tested, and like Job we never gave up. We were U.S. Marines.

I had walked into a deep, I thought broad, hillside ditch that reminded me of the sunken road that played a part in the battle of Fredericksburg during the Confederate War. The sides of this ditch were lined with wounded men who had been shot down when they had charged up the wooded hill just a few yards the other side of a narrow strip of growing wheat. We were greeted by a hatless, jacketless, well-built major who had his sleeves rolled above his elbows. He was literally in a rage. He had been ordered to take the hill, presumably at the request of the French command, who hadn't as yet left all our local movements in the control of our on-the-spot officers. This hill contained a large number of boulders with German machine gun barrels sticking out from their almost impregnable position. Such an attack, to be successful, required special preparation and munitions that had not been given the major and he was "damn mad about it." They had ordered us to do what the major thought, and later proved to be, an impossible task, and to make a useless sacrifice of men. Whereas if proper preparations

101

and right strategy had been followed at first, as was later done, the hill could have been taken with comparatively few losses. Thus, the enraged major, popping his fist in the palm of his hand, walked up and down the gully, yelling his explosive language. He was not our battalion major, but I knew him by reputation. I had seen him in action. He was hard boiled, he was a man's man, and really did care for his men and their welfare. He was not putting on a make-believe show. He was, in his own words, "ordered to send men to hell," and he did not like it and wanted us to know it.

In the face of this background of wounded men who lined the sides of the road-like ditch, and who had tried and failed to do what we were ordered to do, and in full knowledge of the hopelessness of the situation, spurred on by the major's remarks. We, to the last man at the major's order, "GO!," climbed over the top of the ditch, lined up and were on our way to carry out an impossible assignment.

We were in close-order skirmish line formation. We made our way through the wheat, entered the small tree woods, and from there on I could see only a few feet to my right or left. Until I had reached an opening on the German side, where the underbrush had been cleared away in order to make an ideal place for their guns to sweep the hillside, my knowledge of our advance was limited to twenty or thirty feet either way and I am a witness of only that short part of a long line of men.

While in the trees, I could see nothing to shoot at and was not fired upon. I passed on out into the open and still had no target or indication of the location of the Germans. When I had advanced a short distance in the direction I thought toward the German position, the bullets started coming my way like a swarm of wasps when their nest has been disturbed. There was no ditch, hole or coverage of any kind near me, so I hit the ground at body length with my head toward the position of the machine gun. I saw no target to fire on. The gunners were too well hidden for that. I am positive, judging from the sound of the bullets and the dirt kicked up around me, that at least two machine guns were covering the part of the hill and sending bullets in my direction. One gun was sending bullets probably waist high and above my body, the other one aimed lower and was sweeping the ground to get soldiers lying stretched out as

I, and the proper position for one to be in who wished to pick off the gunners with rifle fire. Those passing above would hit me only if I raised up, so it was the lower ones that I watched with fear and interest. I knew where they were hitting for I could see the dirt kicked up by them. The bullets knocking up dirt that was in line with my head appeared to be getting closer and I kept wondering where the next one would hit. Of course I was scared, who wouldn't be? No excitement, just plain scared to move. Lay still, watch and wait, is what I did. Maybe my muscles were paralyzed, I don't know. Anyway, that was the right thing to do. Any movement visible to the gunner might cause him to hold the gun on me, which would have meant a quick end to my life. You can't run; you can't fight back ; it isn't a contest; there is no sportsman's thrill in being a still target against such odds. You just have to wait it out and I am telling you, brother, that while the waiting period may be only minutes, time passes slowly at times like this. When the pop, whisp and buzz grow faster and louder and the digging bullets get closer and closer you think it'll never stop. Strange to learn, but up close like this the pops are separate and distinct, whereas farther away the separate noises blend together and make a roar. Like thunder, when close it is loud clap, at a distance it's a roar.

After seemingly a long, long time, from down the line word is passed from man to man (how we heard it, don't ask me, maybe our intuitive and subconscious mind pickup the message). From whom? After it was all over no one would admit ordering a retreat. Apparently, Sergeant O'Kelley who was leading my platoon couldn't have given the order. He was brought down with three or more bullets in his body and left for dead in the most advanced part of the line. I do not have the answer. The order that drifted down to me was, "When the machine gun fire holds up get back to the trench." It never occurred to me what might happen to our poor behinds when we charged with our backs to those deadly machine guns. Anyway, we didn't care a dinky ding for where we were, obeying orders was second nature to us, so why not leave? Well, the bullets stopped coming as suddenly and as completely as they had begun. As one man, we had the order, and obeyed it. We were up and literally flew back down that hill and into our ditch. Why I do not know, but not a shot was fired into our backs. Why should the Germans stop shooting in the first place? I do not know. Who gave the order for our retreat remains a mystery. To all these questions, I wish to add my own.

"How in the hell would the one who gave the order know the Germans would hold their fire, and not mow us down when we rose to our feet?"

Our losses were extremely heavy. The Germans, at our request, permitted us to return and bring out our wounded. Sergeant O'Kelley of Alabama was left up there because we thought he was dead. But more than a year later I learned that he was picked up by the Germans, carried to a hospital and after the close of the war returned to his home. While it is against my policy to single out individuals and write about them – perhaps it being Sunday morning has something to do with it – my wish is to say this of Sergeant Craver O'Kelley, Company G, Sixth Regiment Marines. He was in my opinion the most dedicated Christian sergeant I ever met. An official military report, in part, had this to say:

"Proved himself a non-commissioned officer of sterling worth in the operation against the enemy on the 6th and 8th of June. Cool and skillful under fire, he was a tower of strength to his command during the assaults on machine gun positions against great odds. This brave soldier was killed in the performance of his duty."

I was not near enough to see the sergeant while attacking the machine gun position so will write as it was told to me. This sergeant, when brought down, was out front of his platoon a few yards from and facing a machine gun with its barrel sticking out of a small opening between large rocks or open space between parts of a boulder. The Germans behind those rocks could not be picked off with rifle or pistol fire, neither could we charge and cut them down with our bayonets. Hand grenades, yes, but for that assault we had none. My guess and speculations are no better than yours. But perhaps it could have been this way. Sergeant O'Kelley was the kind of soldier that would not or could not turn his back and run from an enemy. But he had done all in his power to do, he was down deadly wounded, there was no chance of his men succeeding and further efforts would merely mean useless sacrifice of his men, and before passing out he gave the order to retreat. Perhaps the one that heard it from the sergeant couldn't be absolutely sure he had heard right, and did not want to be burdened with the responsibility of having started the word along, kept his secret. Even an English-speaking German could have started the word along. If you care to do a little speculation of your own keep in mind that we were not shot in our backs while running away, we were permitted to bring out our wounded, the sergeant was picked up by the Germans and carried to a hospital.

Not yet did we know that we had saved Paris from being plundered and humiliated by the Germans. We had not realized the far reaching importance of our local victories. We did not know that our Marine blood that ran so freely in our own and their cause had kindled in others new hope, new courage and a greater will to do and die for the common cause. Neither did we realize that we had set an example for other men to follow and given a challenge that they could not ignore, that we had softened the iron heel and squashed the idea that the German Army was an invincible foe. We did not know that we were heroes. All we knew was the misery that had been administered to us as individuals. The cockiness of our former selves had been smothered under the burden of misery. Our self-esteem was shocked by the assaults upon our physical dignity. The pride in our soldier-like strength, fortitude and the ability to make jokes of our troublesome burdens had dwindled to a very low depth and all that kept us from acting like a whipped pup was that we never forgot that we were United States Marines.

And then a propaganda filled newspaper reached us in the dark woods and spelled out in glorying terms the heroic deeds of the Marines. And believe it or not, we received a transfusing like stimulant that brought a restoration of our old spirit – not all of it, for it would take time for that to happen.

Our self-esteem made a quick return. We brightened up and were ready and did go into the adventure with death in another battle with the bravura of an unconquerable hero and with shouts and laughter as we rolled along in another truck ride to another front and battle. This time the Paris papers had announced that the American Marines would be thrown into the battle lines and before we had any knowledge of where we were going we came into a large-size French town and found the streets were lined with people with newspapers in their hands that had a lot of information about the Marines. The crowd recognized who we were, waved their papers and shouted, this time with the thrill of joy in their voices.

"American Marines! Marines!"

We had won the right to be recognized and the press had given us full and half-page coverage. We were Devil Dogs. We now ranked with their Blue Devils. We were known fighters and not questionable substitutes thrown into line in desperation because we alone were available for the job.

Before leaving the battle of Belleau Wood for good there is a little mopping-up work that should be done. While of little significance in the eyes of the historians, the exploits that happened to the writer, and the little personal things that are of great importance to all soldiers and are not found in school history books, are in line with the purpose of this story. They explain a lot of things the history books leave for the reader to figure out for himself.

Chapter 13

When the Marines went into the line on June first, my battalion, the Second of the Sixth Regiment, took over that part of the front line that extended from the Paris-Metz road through Triangle Farm to Lucy on the northwest. My company was left out of the line and put in support of it. Which meant that we were held in readiness to go into the line when and where needed. It also meant that some of us could be and were used to carry ammunition and other supplies to the fighting units and to perform what other services were needed.

Our first casualties in my company in the Belleau Wood area came on June second, I believe it was at Triangle Farm, which was sitting straddle a stone-surfaced road and surrounded by a high stone wall. The dwellings and farm buildings were joined up with the wall with a good size space or court in the middle forming what in Georgia we would call the barnyard. Its outside entrance was through a road-wide gateway to the outside. We had moved into the farm the night before and part of my company had been billeted in an animal, perhaps feeding barn. The floor was covered with straw upon which we slept. The upper-end buildings and wall protected us from stray German machine gun bullets. As I remember it, our front line was only a short distance from our quarters. The Germans had advanced so rapidly that the farm owner had left behind several nice dairy cows and a drove of hogs that were running loose about the farm.

At the time we moved into the place, it was thought that the Germans had not brought into action in that section any artillery. So at that time, it seemed to be a good location for our company. But it wasn't to remain like that for long. A small group of fellows and I were idling away the time standing outside the temporary quarters of a doctor and dressing station. The doctor was standing just outside his quarters and more or less blocking the door of the stone building when a shell came over and landed near us. It was close, and naturally when we heard it coming and realized that it was going to land in the barnyard, we dived for the entrance to the building. The doctor's reflexes were slower than ours, or probably he hadn't received as much practice dodging shells as we. Anyway

107

his body blocked the entrance to the building and I was shocked at the curse words one fellow blared out at the situation in general but mostly, as we could tell, directed at the M.D. who simply ignored the man's cursing.

While this was taking place a goodly number of Marines carrying ammunition were approaching the farm down the road some three hundred yards away. While we were watching them, shells begin to drop among them and as we watched we saw several of them go down and it looked as if the most of them would be hit and the wounded lying in the road would be killed if they were not quickly removed and put under cover. All this happened much quicker than it takes to write it. The doctor, addressing us, said, "Those men need help." I was willing to go to their aid so with all the elegance at my command replied, "Sir, I for one will go." A challenge, I felt sure, would make every one there follow my lead. I turned on my heels and at a fast trot made for the farm gate through which the road entered the rock wall enclosed farm.

As I went through the gate along a rock surfaced road, the warning came that another shell was falling fast and my reflexes took over and when the shell hit the spot where I had been a few seconds previous, I was in a squatted position in the bottom of a four foot ditch that ran along the side of the road. When the rock and spent pieces of metal blown up by the exploding shell ceased falling on and around me, I eased up and peeped out over the top of the ditch. I saw coming toward me running madly and blindly another soldier. I instantly realized that all that runner could see was the ditch and if I didn't move quickly that a hundred and sixty pound chunk of human weight following tough hob-nailed brogans would land on top of my head. My trained reflexes again took over and I was able to dodge and escape the threatened injury.

I continued on down to the ammunition carriers and the thing I remember best about this incident is that while working with the wounded I came face to face with our company's former lieutenant who had been left behind in the States because he had taken the measles while on furlough at home and was unable to accompany us overseas. Our greetings were limited to the exchange of smiles. I don't recall very much of my activities the rest of the day, but do know, whatever they were, they kept me from the farm several hours and that when I returned, hogs were out there at the entrance gate and I was made a little sick at the sight of seeing a bunch of hogs with their snouts pushing through minute pieces of human flesh and blood. We lost five men killed there that day.

On my return I found that my company had moved out of the barn and the men were digging in mother earth and were establishing grave-shaped holes for a place to hide and escape from the shells. The men were paired off in two to a hole, and as long as they stayed in their place in their hole it was their private property and no one was permitted to challenge their right to this small part of the wooded area. They slept and rested in their holes when there were no duties or assignments to require their presence elsewhere.

I believe it was the same day late at night I was on a chow detail and going back into the barnyard I found some food supplies had been delivered and our first lieutenant was in charge of issuing them out and it was my lot to carry some of them to some of the boys on the firing line. As I think of that night, it occurs to me that our office boys remained in one of the farm buildings and I was able to bum them out of a cup of coffee that they had made in the farmer's kitchen.

During any tragedy and especially during a hard serious war, Christians and a lot of others who are not good Christians, do a lot of praying and in the past people have questioned me on that subject. While I cannot answer for all of the individuals that made up my outfit, I can and will answer for myself and others I have observed and questioned on the subject.

Generally speaking, soldiers ask God to help them, only when they feel helpless and cannot help themselves. I doubt seriously if one ever prays for help in killing of the enemy or for victory. These are things a soldier must do for himself. I have not observed anyone praying before going into battle or while they were actually physically engaged in the act of fighting.   Certainly, faith in God, in your buddies, your officers, your fighting unit, your country and yourself are so great in magnitude that one could not fight at all if all of them were missing. A little faith helps a little, a lot of faith helps a lot is the way I see it.

Since there are good praying people on both sides, how can prayer help any soldier? My answer to this question is a story of my own experience and I will leave it to you to say whether or not my prayer was answered and if a miracle was performed for me. This true story will come later. I want to get you in a thinking mood before I present it to you.

Let's begin by saying that men are animals and that there are kindred characteristics and physical similarities between the human and the beast. Man is, of course, a superior animal, but it is hard to find any given trait possessed by man, cat or dog that isn't possessed to some degree in each of the three, man, cat, dog. Each can express joy and grief, hate and devotion, anger and friendliness, fear and boldness. The four-footed animals cannot speak our language, neither can we speak theirs. But there is a lot we can learn by studying our four-footed friends.

A rooster, cat, dog or man will fight bolder and show more courage in his or its own backyard, because he or it feels more secure there. We American soldiers in France felt more secure under the command of our American officers than under a French officer even though we knew that the French one had had more training, more experience and more knowledge of the country than our officers. Faith in your buddy, captain, country or God gives one a sense of security which will add to his fighting ability.

Faith in God is a kind of superstructure and protective shield non-believers do not have. It, too, has its limitations, and anyone who asks for too much is bound to be disappointed. It is not a magic that will give all one might ask for.

A lot of us were approaching the end of our ability to stand any more trials, tribulations or shocks. But more were to come. The first notice we received that death and destruction were again coming our way was a warning frightful shriek of a descending shell that let us know that we had only seconds in which to seek protection from the hot blast of flying parts of an exploding shell. From its speed of approach, the shock of its shriek, and the sharp whisk sound it made as it came near, it appeared to me that fate had selected me for this one's victim. It landed only a few feet away. Dirt, hot pieces of iron and rock fragments rained down on me. My hole buddy hadn't had

110

time to return to our hole, so I was alone in our scooped out, grave-like hole. As if the first shell was only a warning of what was to follow, other shells came on thick and fast. Roar after roar followed until the earth trembled, the air became hot and thick with dust, smoke and gas fumes, and shell fragments. Out of the smoke-filled darkness came cries for help and shrieks as men were hit. Some of the most deadly wounded, died.

When a man is put through a continuous physical strain of performing a task that requires him to labor over and beyond his normal capacity for work, his body rebels and loses its power to function properly. Man's nervous system, mind and emotions work in a similar pattern. The physical body requires rest and time to recuperate from overwork. The same is true of the mind and moan's emotions. Literally, we Marines in the Belleau Wood were exhausted in body, mind and spirit.

It is not uncommon in war for one to become so completely exhausted that he cannot stand any further drain on his emotional power to survive. Some give up and become prisoners of war and even traitors to their country. Some apparently aid in their own destruction by foolishly walking into the enemy's fire when such an act serves no good purpose. Some are what is called shell-shocked.

Insanity does not affect all individuals in the same manner. Some are harmless, some kill themselves, while others attack and murder members of their own family. I have seen a sergeant weep, heard a private curse a captain to all kinds of names. I have known of a real successful fighting major pulling a ridiculous absurd stunt, of a hard boiled captain that had to take a rest from his company, a private who stood up and shook his fist at a German machine gun and one guy who thought our return voyage would last forever, he had lost all hope of ever returning home.

A lot of want and a lot of need make a simple product a thing of great value. So you will excuse me for using one mess kit filled with common beans, a chunk of bacon, American punk and coffee sufficient reason for telling another tale that started one late night in the woods. We were returning from one of our missions of woe, tired and pretty near fagged out. A buddy and I were the tail end of the line. The night was about spent and we were sure that we would

111

not make another move that night. We were halted and we thought the company was moving in position to select holes where we would finish out the night and spend the day. Being last in line all the best holes would be taken before we could get in the place, so we thought it okay to step out of line and find a good hole, crawl in it and go to sleep. We quickly found a satisfactory hole and were soon sound asleep. When we awoke the next morning the company was nowhere around. They were gone from that part of the woods and we had no idea where they were. The only sensible thing for us to do was to find and report to our battalion headquarters and report that during the darkness of the previous night we had gotten lost from our company and ask for directions for finding it. We found the headquarters and while waiting for a runner who would accompany us as far as Major Garret's post from which later a runner would accompany us to the new location of our company, we had some time to wait and I used this time to hunt up a field kitchen, washed my face and hands and was served a mess of beans, bread and coffee. The first coffee and warm cooked meal I had eaten in the Lord knows when. A meal I can never forget because it was the most wanted in a lifetime.

The major did not ask us any embarrassing questions of why we were not with our company, as some officers would have done. Getting lost in the woods was logical and reasonable, but deliberately stepping out of line was bad business and we kept that to ourselves. The major was very nice and considerate to us. He was more like a father or friendly uncle than an old fighting major. I was very much impressed by his ability to make us feel at home there in his presence. I left there in better spirits than I had enjoyed in a long time, a good cooked meal and hot coffee, a day away from my company and the battlefront, combined with a friendly visit with an old time major was a real tonic for me and I am sure my buddy experienced the same feeling as I. It seems that there ought to be a way to arrange breaks for all soldiers in a fierce fighting front.

Some of the Marines, in fact most of them, had been in the woods for fifteen days without sufficient water to wash their hands. Certainly these men had no idea or intention of quitting, but there comes a time when the bravest of men endowed with sterling qualities of physical strength and self-endurance reach a stage of fatigue when something had to be done for their relief. The French custom under similar circumstances was to relieve their soldiers after the fourth or fifth day. "But no," the French officer said to our American commander, "those Americans are young fellows, leave them there." As a last resort, and a risky thing to do, our commander sent into the woods men from an American division that had not finished its training. A lot of them probably sent across to boost the morale of the French people and build up material for the American propaganda machine.

If these men had been brought into Belleau Wood quietly, placed in their holes and told to keep under cover and shoot like hell if the Germans started an attack, it is very probable that this green battalion, many of whom only six weeks previous had been sworn into the service and some few had not fired a rifle, could have held the line without mishap, and given the Marines a chance to take a bath, get caught up with their sleep, and then go back into the line refreshed.

"No," said, that noble French officer, whose decorated breast left no room for another medal and whose personal dignity and exalted self-esteem would not allow him to seek information from the roughneck Americans in the line. In total ignorance of the local situation he gave orders for these green troops to attack. The result was disastrous. The poor, unschooled, bewildered men were like helpless babes in a darkened forest and if the Germans had been fully aware of the real situation they could have picked up their packs and walked back in full possession of all of Belleau Wood. Fortunately, the Germans did not know this and the Marines were immediately sent back into the woods. The green troops were sent back and given some hard practical training and according to later reports developed and proved themselves capable and successful soldiers.

The unfinished business of clearing the woods of the Germans was still on the books and this time the job was turned over to the Third Battalion of Marines. This time there would be victory. This time proper preparations were made and proper strategy was used and though there were plenty losses the Germans lost more heavily than we and victory was ours.

I was not in the attacking party but following the successful attack our company went in and took a front line defense position in the captured territory.

When my line halted near an overhanging large rock, my foxhole buddy and I latched onto this place as our future hole and home. It had been some German's hole before the attack and it was evident that whoever they were, they had to leave in a hurry. They had left three brand new rifles that had never been shot and a lot of ammunition that fitted the rifles. While the Germans were in use of the hole the opening under the overhanging rock or ledge faced their own rear and it was a perfect protection from our artillery fire, now the mouth was facing the German front, which made it not nearly as safe for me as it had been for the German occupants.

However, at that, it was preferable to an open-top foxhole, especially if it were to start raining. My buddy and I got out our tools and started digging the hole under the rock deeper to increase its depth and thus make it more secure from shell fire. The deeper we dug the stronger the stink that came from the bottom of the hole. So we stopped digging for the night. The thought had come to us that the stink very well could be coming from a decaying body of a dead soldier and we would forego any further digging until daylight.

With the coming of another day we continued digging and improving our hole. Almost everyone along the line was busy doing the same to their foxholes. Experienced soldiers do not have to have someone standing over them telling them what to do; the corporals, sergeants and lieutenants can be digging their own holes and preparing their own quarters. If the outfit that preceded us had a prepared machine gun position or officers' position it is expected that our gunners and officers will move into these prepared positions. In our company, logic, reason and fairness as well as military courtesy and law prevailed and governed our conduct.

After a couple of feet we came to a buried sack and found that the stink came from parts of a limburger cheese. The sack also contained a letter a German had written to his wife and two children back home in Germany but hadn't had time or an opportunity to mail. Then, too, there were three other letters that he had received from his family. We were curious to know what this fellow had written his wife and what the little woman had to say to her husband soldier. One of our neighbors who could read Dutch read them to us. The letters were as anyone should expect. They were no different from what any American Christian wife or soldier would write each other. From the wife was a statement that she and the children were praying for the safety of her husband. He expressed hope that the dreadful war would soon be over and asked God's blessings for his family.

We arrived in the place close behind the retreating Germans and had to prepare our line of defense. Ordinarily, we could expect that the Germans would immediately organize a counterattack and we had to get ready to defend ourselves.

Our first task was to prepare our customary foxholes on the hillside, that is if one couldn't find one already dug and left there by the preceding forces. Our next task was to go down to the bottom of the steep but small ridge or hill and dig rifle pits which were dug at the edge of the trees. At night we manned the pits, and maybe a few spent the day there. During the day most of us stayed and slept in our ridge-side holes. I don't think anyone was supposed to sleep at night. We certainly did not remove any of our clothes. We did not know day or night at what time the Germans might put on a raid or attack. In the daytime we would have time to arouse the men, but at night they could be almost on top of us before we had any warning. Our position was on the upper end of the woods, on the north west side of the ridge. Part of the village of Belleau, I think it was, was almost directly in front of the way my hole under the rock faced. Though the hillside was a wooded area, the front of my place was wide open and I had a perfect view of the small village and a road that came down a hill and entered the village from the bank. While the Germans in the village were completely hidden from my sight, soldiers using the road at its back were in plain view for more than four hundred feet.

The shade and shadows of the overhead limbs were some help in hiding my place, and the large rock at its back cut off and prevented a skyline view from the enemy and some limbs in front on the newly dug dirt offered some protection from the eyes of the enemy. Nevertheless, none of us doubted but that a trained spotter could find the place with the aid of his field glasses. I was kidded by other fellows for setting up a perfect target for the German gunner to aim at. My response to this kidding was that no German could hit the mouth of my dugout and that they were at just the right distance from me, fifteen to twenty feet, to be hit by shells aimed at my dugout.

One day I was sent away from our position on some errand and on my return found that, sure enough, the enemy had spotted my dugout and had fired a half dozen shells at it and as I had predicted most of them missed it by fifteen to more feet and fell close to my neighbors who were in their holes, but one of their dang small shells did go right through the mouth of my place and played havoc with its insides. Lucky me, if I had been there at the time they would have had to pick up the many pieces and bury me in a sack. Did I move out? Heck no! I had a theory for almost everything and one was that shells, like lightning, rarely strike twice in the same place.

Though we were shelled many times, it was nothing like what we had suffered previously. We now had plenty drinking water, more to eat and dog biscuits to gnaw on. We knew where the Germans were and could see out and had little fear of a sudden surprise attack. And believe it or not, our position in this place was such an improvement over the others that we came close to enjoying it there. My biggest cause for discomfort was not shells, bullets or fear of the Germans, but a case of dysentery. One day while I was in the throes of a dysentery move some distance from our inhabited holes, hunting for a new and clean place to squat (from the looks of things the Germans we drove out of the woods also suffered from dysentery) , the darn Germans started dropping shells in the area. Instead of giving up in despair and feeling sorry for myself, I really saw the humor in the situation and yelled to my buddy to tell those blank to blank Germans to cut out their shelling:

"I want to ----"

My hole was waist-deep below the ground in front of it and from the ground to the top where the rock extended out in front, which made it a kind of ledge, some four feet above the ground level. I called this opening the mouth to my hole or dugout. Generally speaking, I spent my daylight time there and did all my sleeping in the dugout.

At night, I usually would go down the hill and stand watch in a rifle pit. One of my favorite pastimes during the day when I had caught up with my sleep, was to stand and gnaw on a hard tack, which we called dog biscuits, for that's what they looked like and for all I know that's what they tasted like. Now don't get me wrong, I don't know how we could have gotten along without them. We simply carried them loose in our pockets and pulled them out and gnawed on them as a pup would gnaw on his bone. They were practically water and mold proof ; therefore, preferred to American loaf white bread if it had to be carried any length of time. The American bread would mold quickly when carried in our pockets or kept in a trench or dugout.

One day while idling my time away just standing there gnawing on a dog biscuit during a quiet period, while almost everyone else was in deep slumber on the hillside, and maybe a few fellows scattered here and there were in the rifle pits, I was shocked into the full wakefulness of an alert soldier, for not more than two hundred feet away was a fully dressed German, with full marching pack and rifle. His rifle was hanging at his side with the strap slung over his shoulder. Not a voice of objection was raised, not a stir among our men could be seen or heard, apparently only my eyes were open seeing that we had a live, armed German in our midst. I am sure that this was no dream or nightmare. I was wide awake and it was broad daylight. I was standing in arms length of my loaded rifle, a bullet in its place in the gun and ready to be shot. The target was so close that I couldn't have missed at that distance. Did I shoot? No! Why not? Because that would have been murder. Like shooting a man in his sleep. He was walking along within a few yards of a dozen of our men as unconcerned and indifferent to his danger as if he had been walking down the main street of his home village. How he got there I have been unable to figure out. He was of no danger to us. He was lost. I yelled, "Capture that German." He sprang to life and in seconds my view of him was cut off by the trees and I didn't learn what happened to him. He could have gotten completely away for not many men like to shoot a peaceful man in his back.

Standing in the same position, under almost identical circumstances another incident took place. This time it was one of the German daredevil plane observers who paid us a visit. He was not lost and he was on war business, which made him fair game for any man's rifle and it would have been soldier business and not murder to have placed a bullet in his body and stop his fighting career. Did I do it? No! Why not? Well, I will answer that question, though it is no credit to me that I let slip this one opportunity in a million to have been recognized as a hero of World War One for having done a deed so rare that I have never heard of it having been done during the whole war.

He came from my rear flying over my rock just over the tops of those medium tall trees. Then in the open between the trees just in front of my stand where there was a broad open space he banked his small plane, brought it almost to a stand still with the plane's nose pointed at a forty-five degree angle upward, actually bent over the plane's cockpit and gazed down at our rifle pits, straightened out his plane and was gone. How many seconds it took for all this to happen? Probably about the same it takes for a covey of quail to make its turn. Any crack shot sportsman with his wits about him could have made a kill. Not less than two-thirds of his head and body were in full view not more than two hundred feet away, long enough for the airman to lean over and take a look at the ground and our rifle pits. But I was not a crack shot, sportsman, and neither did I have my wits under control; I was in shock with surprise. My lady luck had left me for a time. Probably Sergeant York with his mountain experience in hunting wild turkeys and tree squirrels could have pulled the stunt, but not me.

Our relief came; we were leaving; this was for good. Only in my memory and by visionary trips would I again walk the dangerous trails that dodged here and there between the trees and rock like boulders and remember that these were our woods, Marine Woods. I was tempted to drop to my knees and in prayer ask God's blessings upon the wandering spirits of our dear comrades that we were leaving behind, their bodies buried in the cold, cold earth. But, no! It could be that they were in the enlightenment that comes with the Crossing of the Bar – have moved into another sphere where peace, goodwill and painless fellowship exist between the spirits of man. Who am I to cast doubts upon the destiny of men who gave their lives for a cause in which they believed? I do not believe a single one of these men killed in hate. They definitely were not murders. They fought for the good of their country. The guilty persons in war are the people who make the leaders who make the war and not the poor fellows that have to bear the burden and hardships of the battle lines.

Chapter 14

As previously stated, it was my practice to leave the kitchen crew and join the fighting squads each time the company headed for a new fighting front. But thinking the outfit would be heading for some easy support position, rest or training camp, I did not do so when they boarded camions (French buses) and headed for Forest De Retz. My usual line squad leader I served with while in the ranks previously would inform me when we were headed for a fighting front. But he failed to do so this time. It is possible he had a full squad without me, my place having been taken by a new recruit. Again, since ours was a surprise move, few if any of the non-commissioned officers knew where we were headed. If they had, I believe I would have been told, and would have joined the fighting forces and rode the camions with them. As it was I was left to trail along behind them when they headed for a new battle front, just a little south of Soissons, and thus missed out on that drive. Instead I caught a ride, at least part of the way on a supply truck.

When the plans call for moving two hundred thousand men, with artillery and supplies into a forest without the enemy knowing about it, you have to do a lot of moving under cover of darkness without lights. That means slow going, many accidents and road jams. And when you mix in the traffic horse-drawn water carts, mule-pulled heavy machine guns, truck-hauled supplies, horse cavalry, tanks, touring cars and walking soldiers you have a problem that only military genius and power would undertake to solve. And as if all this were not enough to produce sufficient confusion, the camions were driven by Chinese and one division on the road were Africans. There were French, Scots, Americans, Chinese and Africans that spoke different languages and dialects, each in his native tongue yelling to the world that by right of necessity he must have the right of way. The chaos, mix-ups and confusion were more like a mad crazy nightmare than a real mass of human beings trying to get to the same place. How such a snarled, entangled mass of humans could right itself, separate, and the different groups get its many parts organized into a working machine with each part fitted in where it belong at the front, seemed impossible to me. Like the hands, springs, cogs and screws of a gigantic clock, each little part had its place and every part was vital to the proper operation of the whole works. To say it works like a clock is the highest compliment that can be given any team. This battle didn't and very few others ever earn that compliment. The diversity of parts made the task of this battle more difficult and required twice the energy to perform than it would have taken if there had not been such a conglomeration of differences in the separate units that were quickly thrown together to fight the battle.

To me personally it is significant and worth recording though some of the Marines had to trot the last two hundred yards, they did make it to the fighting stage on time and the show started promptly as scheduled at four forty-five a.m., July 18, 1918. Believe it or not, these Marines who had been on the move, riding the hard plank seats of a jolting truck, and walking mile after mile with little to eat, scarcity of drinking water, and part of the time lost in the dark, had to trot to the jumping off place. Not only filled their sector in the line and advanced the several miles to reach their prescribed objective, but on the way an African bunch, probably close to a French division of Moroccan infantry on their flanks, began flagging and the Marines and soldiers from the American First Division were forced to extend their lines and assume the extra burden and carry forward the advance of the section of the line allotted to the African troops.

While my brave buddies were being killed by the Germans and were suffering every pain known to the physical body, including hunger and thirst, this chow hand was miles behind, worrying about the safety of his friends, lonesome for the gang and ashamed of himself for being left in the rear. The chow hand was not a brave man, but his pride shamed him when he didn't act like one.

Right now, what happened on the way up to the battle front does not seem to be very important. Anyway, the best I can record here about this trip is that the noise and continuous roar put my tired body and mind to sleep and I slept so soundly that I have no recollection of the time, or things that happened toward the end of the journey. My consciousness and memory of things goes to me in the forest after we arrived there and starts with me a few yards behind several French 210 artillery guns and where I felt the earth's vibration each time they fired a round of shots. I noticed that my right shoulder was sore, and on examining it I found that where it had come in contact with the truck's rough floor it had been rubbed raw. This happened while I was asleep and shows how soundly I slept as our truck nosed its way through the noisy, tangled road jams.

The Forest De Retz served well as a hiding place for troops but my short stay in it didn't prove to be much fun. The tall hardwood trees were instruments of destruction and whirlwinds of panic while I was in there. The pop and cracking split that preceded a downward crash that followed the yell, "Timber," made us rear hounds that lingered there jump and run for our lives as the trees came crashing to earth. The thorough Germans, the know-how Boche, had placed dynamite in the trunks of those trees and as they retreated set off the blast, to block the way and handicap the American troops that were following them.

Many of the blasts did not bring the trees immediately to the ground but left them tottering as if they were undecided on when or in what direction to follow in their fall. Many others had been dangerously slashed by large shells and were left standing waiting for a little nudge to bring them down. The engineers who were right there with the fighting boys no doubt have nightmares of horror whenever they remember their toils in clearing the forest roads of the large dynamited trees. But there were a lot of them left to bedevil us and though the night's darkness had eased from the woods, a ghostlike breeze would mingle with their tops and another tree would come crashing down. There was no telling which tree would fall next. Just one at a time, here and there, some kind of fate would make the decision and another tree would give up the struggle and follow the general pattern.

After a time, as we could no longer hear the bursting of shells on the front and the French had stopped firing their field pieces, we judged it time for us to move out and start hunting for our boys on the firing line. We had no maps and there was no one near from whom we could get any reliable information. We just followed a road that we thought went in the direction our men had taken.

We passed by two downed and partly destroyed fighting planes, further on we stopped where a battery of German "Big Boys" had been left by the Germans for our forces to salvage. We trailed along where the road came to some homes and were hailed from one of them by a couple of young fellows who kept our company's records. These company clerks would ordinarily know where the fighting members of our company could be found, but not this time. Going further along the road, we came to a real sunken road. There were several soldiers idling there and one gave a rather dramatic picture of a German plane that had flown rather low up the road with its machine gun going full blast strafing the men in the road, and while these men were full of talk none could give us any information of our company. We had reached a point where the road made a turn and from a high point on the ridge though we could see in the distance the fighting front. We decided it was time to leave the road and start walking through the open country, but were puzzled what direction to take. Here we ran across a lieutenant that had recently joined our company but he, too, was lost from the company and could not give us the desired information we were seeking. Then we met a Marine not of our company who informed us that all the Marines on the front would be relieved that night. We then gave up our hunt and returned to our field kitchen that had been set up on the side of the road some distance back.

The company came in as expected. They had had it tough and their loss was heavy. Many had been lost from the company as was the lieutenant. There was so much evidence of close fellowship and closeness of personal feelings between each other and their remaining officers, who stuck together through it all, that I, fully aware of their hardships and the experience in the battle, couldn't help but envy them of their experience. It has been demonstrated to me time and again that suffering has its own rewards, and that ease and pleasure exact a heavy penalty.

My memory at this late date is too unreliable to deal in personalities in this manuscript. I could easily get the facts mixed. All the officers that went across with the original company were tops, and remarks made about one of them could very well apply to all of them.

It was my privilege to carry one of our captains who was wounded back from the front. I have forgotten his name. One captain threatened to shoot me. I have forgotten his name. As you realize, it would be bad business to guess at which officer was which in the two incidents.

I am pretty sure that the men in each platoon in our original 80th Company would have picked their own lieutenant as the best in the whole Sixth Regiment. I am using Lieutenant John C. Schneider to illustrate and as an example of what our officers were like. He was not lacking in the dignity of a proper officer and yet was one of us in understanding and fellowship and, in that sense, one of the gang. He felt as well as thought. His feelings had depth and were not simply a lot of professional polish or cultivated airs; he didn't need that kind of props. In my imagination I can see him moving in and out among his men with that careless, friendly, indifferent manner that only officers and men who have been through hardships together can feel toward each other in an organization that requires that each advance in rank from private to lieutenant broaden and tighten the distinction between men of different ranks. While no Marine ever expresses love for another man, love is the only word in our language that will truly express my feelings and that of the others in that group toward Lieutenant Schneider. To tell the truth, after my Soissons Retz experience I was ashamed to remain in the chow detail. In no sense of the word was I anxious to kill or be killed, yet to be left out of the adventure at the front and to be shut out from the inner circle of the fighting men was not to my liking. As long as I was filling a dual position of sharing in the danger and hardships at the front and still did not have to do a lot of close-order drilling and take a lot more training between trips to the front and was given the freedom and privileges of a chow hand I was happy and liked my job. But apparently things had changed. I suspected that my place in a fighting squad had been filled by a replacement and only in dire emergencies would I be called back into the ranks. I had a conflict of emotions. I did not want to be pinned down to one small squad nor did I want to lose out and be left out of the big show that was rapidly developing. To me as I saw it, in the future my division or the Marine part of it would be used as special troops, and would be rushed from point to point, to fill key positions in small and big drives as well as dangerous breaks in important front lines, leaving the chow hands in the rear, and it could become the policy in a lot of cases to use on the line only those who had rehearsed and been trained for the new assignment.

As usual, lady luck was working in my interest. Our regimental medical department put out a call for volunteers for first aid men and stretcher bearers. They had suffered many casualties and were resolved to replenish their ranks before the next drive in which they were expecting an estimated seven thousand casualties. Since our regiment was to be in a key position in the drive, we would get a large share of them and needed to take on probably twenty to thirty new men.

The medical group had set up a small camp in the woods where they received applicants for this service. I reported to them and was accepted as a stretcher bearer and my transfer from chow hand was completed. I was to remain attached to my old company and to follow it wherever it went. I was under the general orders of the doctor assigned to my company and specific orders of the Medical Corps man attached to my company. I wore a Red Cross arm band and went unarmed.

Our immediate boss was a peach of a fellow, and our doctor was a nice guy; I had landed another job that was awfully important and one in which I had plenty room to roam here and yon from the front to rear in and out of adventure. Our duties were to bring in the wounded as efficiently and quickly as possible. All of us had had experience dodging death and knew about such things. So the details of our job were left to us, our own initiative and what our company supervisor could teach us. Obviously, after the battle starts a stretcher bearer is practically on his own and his conscience and sense of duty are his guide and boss. In the majority of cases from the time he picks up his first wounded man in a fast-moving advance on the enemy until the drive is over, every person that has authority to give him an order is so occupied with his own personal obligations that the stretcher bearer is left almost on his own. That was the way it was with me in World War I.

Frankly, we did not nor could we keep up with the fast moving Second Division and do as efficient a job of our work as could have been done if we had more and better training for our job, and information pertaining to the location of the evacuation ambulances and the company we were serving. One's company battalion did not advance in a straight line and the evaluation stations often changed as the front advanced and switched its direction. In practically every advance, someone was wounded in the first couple of hundred yards and in some cases the first hundred feet. And if the first of the attack is very successful by the time the first wounded is gotten back to the dressing station and the stretcher bearer is back to the starting point his men are passed on out of sight and only the noise of the battle and the evidence left by the advancing force plus his knowledge and past experience can tell him how he can make contact with his own company. If he comes across a dead or wounded man from his own outfit he knows he is on the right track; otherwise he has to resort to guesswork. Men passing over any kind of territory leave evidence of their having been there, but there remains the problem of what men went that way.

Thus it follows the more separate outfits in the attack and the more successful the advance, the more difficult it became for us to keep in touch with our company. If the advance went in or through a wooded area the task of following it was made more difficult, and if it reached a road we didn't know whether to cross it or to follow the road to the right or left. There were times when the noise would be coming from two directions at the same time. There were times when there was a gap in the line and in that case there was the possibility of going through the gap and winding up on the German side of the line. Remember, we would be in strange territory without maps or any plans of battle. Well, this should give you some idea of the difficulties I had in keeping up with my company and the Race Horse Division, a name given the Second Division because of the rapidity of its advance against the enemy.

Before getting into the big affair the doctors and hospitals were preparing for, I wish to tell a story that is more to my liking. We were in company and squad formation marching along a peaceful road in the cool early morning. A streak of light had shot across a clear sky and the morning light was in the act of blossoming into another day. A magnificent sun hidden behind distant hills had sent a red search beam ahead that showed the pathway his majesty, the

126

sun, was following across the sky. It was during that glorious period when time hangs in a balance and it is neither day or night, when over and above our heads came the blunt crack of fast-moving machine gun bullets. I instinctively hit the ground and my lips formed these words: "What in the hell?" In all my experience, never before had bullets suddenly come out of the calm quiet while we were marching along a public road back of the front lines.

Why over our heads? Why did the fire from the machine gun fail to come with a sweeping clatter that in seconds could have cut our closed ranks down like a scythe flashing through a stand of wheat? Apparently, as I see it, it couldn't have been any other way than when we got to our own front lines our people let us pass through without stopping us – as they should have done – leaving us to march on to the German line; and they, not seeing us, permitted us to continue on down the road until we came in sight of a support German machine gun. It was not good daylight, they were not expecting us there. We could have been Germans returning from their own front. That shot was a warning from a German gunner who could not tell for sure whether we were friend or foe. Anyway you put it, luck was on our side. By the time I had gotten my wits straightened out, the officers up front of the column had gotten the men in combat formation and were charging up the hill from which the machine gun fire had come.

The other first aid man who carried the stretcher with me and I – not seeing any wounded men in the road – lit out after our fellows who were charging the machine gun and hill and came across a man who had been hit in the leg. We bandaged his leg, dragged him under some bushes and told him to lay low (he was not badly hurt). In front of us were thick, small trees and underbrush that one could see through only a short distance. By this time our men were out of sight. The little and scattered noise they were making was such that we couldn't locate them so had to guess at the direction they took after entering the woods.

We took off in the direction we thought they most likely had gone and came to a line trench the Germans had started digging. It was wide enough but they had dug it only about eighteen inches deep. The underbrush and trees were cleared out and the shallow trench made easy and fast walking there possible. We could not see

127

more than a few yards either to the right or left. Thinking our men had gone in that direction we hurried along it. It appears now that we had gone around the flanks of our men and moved in between the two forces. Each of the two sides were quietly waiting for the other to reveal itself in the thick underbrush. The Germans must have heard my buddy and me, for they started shooting in our direction. We flattened ourselves out in the bottom of the shallow trench. The shots from the Germans gave their position away to our boys and they opened up across the shallow trench and there we first aid men lay while bullets from the two forces came flying over our bodies. A very unpleasant place to be; fortunately for us, neither side had any hand grenades to start tossing at each other. It wasn't long before our boys advanced up to us and their greetings were, "What in the hell are you boys doing here?" Such things are not timed, but shortly we had the area cleared of the Germans.

Having gone around our flanks, I hadn't witnessed much of what had taken place in the woods. A section of our defense lines, where I joined it later, was just inside the woods and faced out toward a typical French walled-in barnyard and stone buildings, to which the Germans had retreated. They were not visible to us while in the buildings or behind the wall of the barnyard. If they had any heavy machine guns at the time I did not see any evidence of them. At this time neither our artillery or theirs were dropping any shells in the immediate area. I presume that neither the Germans or our artillery knew the location of their own or the enemy's troops.

In rambling around in the woods, after it had been cleared of the enemy, I ran across a well-kept, strong dugout with a pleasant setting for a small personal camp. One of our fellows told me that it had been a German quarters and that he thought him a colonel. The German officer was completely surprised and hadn't realized any attack on his position was being made until our boys swamped in on him. We, of course, realized that we had advanced into the German territory and had established a pocket of defense there and only the Lord knew how many Germans were between us and our rear forces. Under the circumstances, we did not immediately start carrying out our wounded or otherwise try to contact the rear. I was told that when our company did not arrive at their designated place on the old front, that our headquarters had a bad case of the jitters. The company had simply vanished – where? Well, no one back there knew, but they were alerted and when the echoes from our little battle on the quiet morning drifted to the rear they guessed what had happened. No details of what was done is known to me. All I know was what happened in my presence. All I can write is what I saw and the fellows told me.

An ex-chow hand or first-aid man is not supposed to be an expert on military affairs. Even so, we recognize swiftness and efficiency along with faultless strategy when we see it, and successful military operation executed without a moment's warning or notice in an unmapped, totally strange terrain is what we saw that morning. The captain gave the first order, but in a situation like this one, the lieutenants, sergeants, corporals and even privates, in the thick brush where visibility is poor, take over and carry the ball. The captain's first order set the pattern for the play and put the ball rolling toward the goal of a quick victory. He could easily have ordered us to take cover on the road and given the Germans in the woods time to get over their surprise and get set for an attack. We would have won eventually starting with that order, but not so easily and with so few losses.

Though unintentional, and by accident, the two stretcher bearers, by causing the Germans to reveal themselves, helped some. Harsh, costly, slowly won victories are the ones that find their way into history books, but it is the easy, quick won battles that this veteran likes to think about.

It is true that the Germans that we met there were not in class with those we met and were to meet in Belleau Wood, Retz, Mont Blanch and several other places I could mention. Then, too, they were surprised, caught off balance and did not have the support of their artillery or the concentration of machine gun fire. We had them outclassed in number and quality of men. Some people are prone to take exceptions as the rule, which makes me a little hesitant to describe the feeble effort of these Germans to make a counter attack on us from the barnyard. There may have been others. This one took place while I was lying prone alongside of the rifle-carrying men at the edge of the woods. No, I did not belong there. The danger was there, but small, my curiosity was big and so I stayed to see and to witness a scene so different from my past experience, I had to see it to believe it.

We had an unobstructed view. We could see the German officer as he persuaded his men to come out into the open field from their hiding place in the barnyard. We could easily tell that the Germans were not experienced, tough fighters. They acted like green recruits and I suspect that's what they were and that this sector, until we barged into it, was a quiet sector and was being used to train fresh recruits. They were gun-shy, timid and did not want to attack. Our men on the firing line knew that they had the Germans outclassed and felt no uneasiness or fear. They lay there enjoying themselves and waited patiently for their officer to get his line started toward us. (If they had been afraid of these Germans they would have started shooting the minute they showed themselves.) You don't wait for a rattlesnake to strike before you take a shot at it.

Then, after their line was formed and they started toward us, the inevitable joke, "wait until you see the whites of their eyes," was voiced here and there along our line, but some itchy finger would press too hard on the trigger of his rifle and with the bang of his rifle every rifle in the line would bang its message, and those timid Germans would go scooting back into the protection of their barnyard. Three times a fruitless effort on the part of the German officer was made to organize a counter-attack. It is my secret thought our fellows were in too good a humor to have tried very hard to kill those poor frightened soldiers. Their frail efforts were so useless, and so revealing of their weakness and lack of strength that I often wonder why any officer under such circumstances would attempt to make an attack facing such odds.

Here I can't but do a little guessing. The German officer didn't really expect to seriously attack our position, he was just giving a bunch of raw recruits a little training. Our men were in too good a humor and it would not have been good sportsmanship to have jumped out there and slaughtered all those weaklings. Perhaps that German officer read us correctly and didn't think he was running too big a risk in doing what he was doing. He may have figured that all of our guns would have taken him as its target if he had used brutal

130

force in getting his men lined up to charge us. It is also possible, and I would guess probable, that he had a machine gun concealed and ready to mow us down if we had rushed out there in that open field and started murdering his small force.

Now don't fool yourself into believing that these Germans were a fair sample of the German Army because they weren't. I doubt seriously that this would have been written if those woods had contained a company of Germany's best, for in that case in all likelihood I would not be around to write it.

We were being relieved and it was time to go. One of our fellows had an injured leg. While not a stretcher case, he needed assistance as he hobbled along. So when the company was relieved from the lines and hiked out by way of the road, I took this crippled soldier and set out at a slow pace across country toward the hospital evacuation aid center. When we arrived there, we found that our doctor and his crew had been relieved by an inexperienced crew of medical corpsmen, and there were four or five times as many there as our outfit had kept in the place. It was after midnight, probably getting close to two o'clock. These new fellows were scattered around asleep lying on top of the ground. At one time when there at the station with a wounded soldier, the Germans had shelled the place unmercifully and I realized that they would do it again. When I realized that they were a bunch of greenhorns and that someone should put them wise to the ways and habits of the German artillery, I began shouting at them, and believe me they came to life in three shakes of a lamb's tail and were all ears to know what was wrong. The poor babes were eager to listen and not bashful about admitting their ignorance and lack of training for the war.

I informed them that the Germans had their artillery trained on their camp, that at any time day or night they might start shelling the place. Also, four o'clock in the morning was the most favorable time to shell. To the question, "What can we do?" I shot back at them, "Find yourself a hole and crawl in it. If you can't find one, dig one and that blank quick. And from here after when you hear a shell coming dive into the nearest hole in sight and keep that up until you become acquainted with the different noises the shells make and can tell whether to stand still, dive in a hole or run for it." I was

131

only an ex-chow hand and stretcher bearer, oh boy! It did my tough old heart good to see privates, corporals and even sergeants jump to the job of digging themselves holes. I was not only saving lives but also teaching this States-trained crew the most important lesson any soldier can learn, namely, how to stay alive.

I managed to get into the small village a little after daybreak. My company had already passed through and was well on its way hiking toward our new home down the road somewhere. With the aid of my big nose, and the knowledgeableness of the ways of the army rolling kitchen, I found it no trouble to track down and find one of the Eighty Third Division's company kitchens. While the cook, who was very anxious to hear from his boys who went up to the lines the night before, was stuffing me with the best his larder could afford and keeping my cup filled with black coffee, I filled him in about the front and his boys. After which I hunted up headquarters and learned where my company was headed and took off leisurely on their trail and thought to myself, "It's great to be a first-aid man with a full stomach and be free to go strolling along a country road in a strange land with no hurry, no worry, just me and my thoughts to accompany me, and the land and new sights to entertain me and maybe dream of a peaceful world after the war and the part I would play in the new drama on my world's stage." For the time I was not shackled by duty, orders or regulations. I was a free man, a happy man, unburdened by duty or obligations or too crowded to enjoy my communion with self.

Chapter 15

America was strong in untrained manpower, money and food. England and France were strong in tanks, planes and guns. So it became a question of bargaining what we had for what they had. General Pershing was ambitious to have his own army, his own front and to use his own strategy, while the French and English wanted to mix our men with theirs under their officers. General Pershing had to depend on the French for planes, tanks and artillery and so could not fight without the cooperation of the French. To get their cooperation he was forced to submit to their demands and was never able to get all the Americans together in one army. From a Frenchman's point of view it would never do to let the Americans have an independent American army in France. The Americans were fresh, eager and bold. The French troops were old, tired and timid (and they had a right to be), but it happened that in every major engagement, and in almost every other affair, the French claimed supervisory power over our forces. Which we resented. It inevitably happened that the American divisions – or when in smaller groups in minor engagements – were used in an attack with French units on their flanks. The Americans advanced more rapidly than the French and had their flanks endangered by the inability of the French to keep up with our fellows. The two forces did not work together any better than would a fast mule teamed with a slow mule in double harness. They blamed us for being too impatient and rash whereas we blamed them for being too slow and too darn careful. We pitied them, they were jealous of us. They wanted our gifts but it made them angry to have to accept charity from those "loud-mouth, boastful, arrogant, roughshod, domineering, ignorant, upstart yanks." (All things considered can one blame them?)

I recall that on three separate occasions we went into French-held trenches for the purpose of going over the top and taking an objective that had previously been allotted to some French forces. My memory has associated these separate occasions with three incidents that linger in my memory and should find a place in this manuscript.

Under circumstances like these there can be no surprise attacks. The attempt by the French to take the strong position was a give-away of the Allies' future plans, and the nature of things required that there would be further attacks. The German soldiers on their front line sit there with their finger on the trigger. Their observers would be trying to spot any movements of troops in the rear. Their short-ranged artillery would be pounding away at all the nearby woods and other places that could provide cover for fresh troops. Attention would be directed at all roads that lead in the direction of the active front. There is nothing quiet or still on a night like this. Maybe we were five or six miles back. We listen to the distant roar of many guns off in the distance and see the lightning-like flash in the sky like that which follows in the wake of a moving thunder storm. One may shiver and wonder what is going on just a few miles away. Very likely the colonel, captain and lieutenants have been briefed on the battle and have been warned that if the French fail in their mission to take the fortified heights, our outfit would be ordered to take over and complete the job that had already cost the French many casualties.

Surely no square mile or less of rough country is worth the lives of hundreds of men? No! But that is not the point. This is the beginning of a big drive to win the war. It has to be gotten out of the way before a frontal attack can be made all along a twenty-five-mile front. Then the order came, the French had admitted defeat. They had tried and lost heavily; they could not make the grade. So we strike out. We have to hustle along and get there in those deep trenches before the Germans lay a heavy, deadly barrage between the attack trenches and their support lines and before our artillery open up on their artillery and base guns, which in itself, would be a dead give-away that we were on our way, like writing them a letter stating that at daybreak we would be charging their lines. We have time, but none to waste. Sweat now means time to cool off later. Fast walking now means less running later. Hastening toward our fate and shortening the time of our arrival could give lady luck a greater opportunity to serve us. We arrive dead tired and everyone knows after strenuous exercise one is ready for sound sleep.

The above words equally describe and report the way it was on three separate trips when we entered seven-foot deep trenches, filled with French soldiers, and made ready to go over the top at the coming of the break of day. The differences between the trips are only in minor detail. They are so similar that at this late date I could not tell which trip led to this or that front and attack.

When we arrived at this one, I was tired and sleepy. The whistling of bullets as they passed over the top of our trench or the shells that occasionally exploded a little to our rear or just in front of us or the moaning of others high in the sky that seemed to roam off to the rear, or the anticipated battle of tomorrow, none of these had any effect on my desire for sleep and rest. The trench contained French soldiers wounded and dead, a fact I was to learn later. The small amount of light that penetrated the trench betrayed the outline of one French soldier with his shoulder slightly propped against the wall of the trench asleep, I thought. Not wishing to disturb him in his slumber, I eased down beside him and decided that his back would make a better prop than the cold bank of the trench, thus in the back to back position sometimes used by hoboes in their camps I immediately went to sleep and did not waken until early dawn.

The early morning time for us to crawl over the top was almost there, the soldiers were stirring around making ready their rifles and other equipment. Having seen to my own readiness to go into action, I reached down and slapped the Frenchman on the shoulder, intending to thank him for serving me as a pillow during the night. The poor fellow fell over and I saw that he was dead. He had died the day before.

In another incident, we arrived a little late. The Germans were acting like they knew that we had arrived and were welcoming us with machine gun bullets and bursting of shells. Some of them were large to be dropping on the front-line trench and there was a probability that some of them contained gas. There was an atmosphere of nervous tension, much more than in the previous incident described. I was just a few steps outside a small group engaged in a serious conversation. It was too dark to recognize faces, only their profiles were visible in the dark trench.

The captain of our company who was among those engaged in the group discussion, turned and faced me and said, "Go tell Lieutenant Black to report to me immediately." I was really temporarily shocked out of my wits. They had runners who kept up with the location of the different parts of the company to run such errands. For me to start off in the dark on such a night hunting for some one I didn't know was not my idea of the duties of a first-aid soldier. Ours was a new captain and it was too dark for him to see my Red Cross band. I thought by ignoring or pretending not to hear the order he would repeat the order maybe to one of the message runners.

Now we were in a dangerous situation, and things had to be done quickly, orders obeyed promptly; explanations and excuses were out of order. The captain had to have absolute control of his men. So when he slapped his hand on his automatic and said, "Damn you, I told you to tell Lieutenant Black to report to me immediately." I was in a tight spot and knew it. I had to make the right response, short and prompt. I couldn't dabble with words or leave any room for the captain to suspect lack of respect for his authority.

My guardian angel was with me. I opened my mouth and these words came out with military snap.

"Sir, who are you?"

"Captain Jones," came back the answer to my question, spoken with telling authority.

Then, from me with military courtesy, "Yes, sir."

I wheeled and was off at a trot. I had had time to think. I quickly located a runner and turned the order over to him, "Captain Jones wants Lieutenant Black to report to him immediately."

Well, what did I think of Captain Jones? I admired and respected the man. Stern, firm enforcement of unquestionable authority was in order. The captain had made an error, being new in the company, an unavoidable one. On the other hand, I not only had the right to know who was giving me the message to carry but it was my duty to know before delivering it. Had I time and reasoned all this out? Of course not. It was my lady luck taking care of me. I have been lucky so often that I have come to believe that an ounce of luck is worth more than a pound of gold any day.

It is embedded in the nature of man and beast to be afraid of new and strange things. I had heard hundreds of bullets whistle across the top of the trenches and hundreds of shells explode outside my trench, and thousands of cracks, whistles and bangs across the country, and seen flash after flash like giant electrical discharges make their blink- and lightning-like flash followed with vibration. When close and directed at you, one can never learn to love it, nor should one cease to fear it. In time one becomes familiar with these things and learns that the noise they make is a kind of warning message. Indeed, noise, like pain, is one of man's best friends. That is, when he learns how to read its message; he knows when to be afraid, when to flee from it and when to ignore it. With this knowledge he develops self-confidence and acts with a clear mind and is not subject to what I call mental paralysis, that is, a condition of the mind that has lost control of its normal functions. It is generally understood that when men's emotions of fear, hate or even sex gain complete control of him he is recognized as being insane. Such a state in man can be temporary or it can be permanent. Lightning is dangerous, thunder is warning, the rainbow is a confirmation of the presence of hope. Nature is a wonderful teacher.

The country rube that has for the first time visited the city is constantly frightened by the city noises, and rolls and tumbles in his city bed as the strange noises drift into his bedroom. The city-bred boy on his first night in the isolated farmhouse is made uneasy by the absence of the city noise and sits up in fright at the hoot of a harmless owl.

The next incident I record took place in a front-line trench from which we would again carry out an assignment already attempted by a French force. It is one of those things we hate to admit did happen in our company but this would not be a true story if I told only the good and admirable things about us. And it contains a type of information raw recruits do not always get in their training camp.

It was necessary to keep someone awake and standing guard in the trench; there was always the possibility that the enemy might take a notion to pull a raid on our trench, or gas be used against us. But the very thing that made the young fellow nervous was our assurance that we were for the time safe from an invasion of our trench by the enemy. For as long as the Germans kept sweeping No Man's Land with machine gun bullets or dropping shells out there in front of us we could rest assured no Germans were on their way to pay us a visit.

Why any corporal would put a lone green replacement on guard who had not previously been exposed to the noise of battle and the activities of a live front trench the night before an attack is to take place is incomprehensible to me, yet that was what someone had done.

Every person among us who did not have a special reason to be up and on the go was taking advantage of an opportunity to be asleep. We were well aware of the fact that we would have it tough all the next day and it could well be that we would not have another chance to sleep in a couple of days. So each time the lonesome, nervous guard would awaken me or my buddy who were sleeping a few feet from the guard's post, we would ball him out for disturbing our rest. It was not my business to give instructions to this guard, though I admit I do feel some guilt for not doing so.

In the stillness of the late night, a few feet from us came the loud crack of a rifle. Almost instantly my buddy and I hit on our feet and in time to hear the death struggle of the shot victim, and to hear in astonishment the nervous guard say, "I got him." We as a matter of course started cursing the guard out for shooting off his rifle in the crowded trench. It could have been a lieutenant and even the captain of our company and us for that matter. Going to the shot soldier we found the guard had killed one of our message runners, a man worth a half dozen green replacements just in from the States. Even if it had been a German, the bayonet or rifle butt and not the firing of the rifle should have been resorted to in close quarters, for shooting up or down that trench endangered the lives of dozens of men. If the barrel of that rifle had pointed at the lower part of the man's body, as it should have been when you shoot at a man only a few feet away, the bullet could have also killed my buddy and me. It is bad enough to have to face the enemy's bullets and it becomes almost intolerable when a soldier has to risk his life to the danger of being killed by his comrades. Such incidents as this receive the hush treatment, mostly because too many people are indirectly involved and must share in the responsibility for letting it happen. Officially, I was innocent of any guilt in this killing, but I realized that by keeping my nose out of other people's business I did not, as I probably could have done, prevent this killing. On the other hand, it is bad business to try to do another man's job. That is the quickest and the surest way I know of for a service man to get into serious trouble. I wasn't above trying it and got by with it too, but a man had better be darn sure he is right when he tries it, and doubly sure that there is no hard-boiled officer around to take issue with him when he does it. All men with lots of authority get mad as the dickens when some little fellow begins to show errors in or find fault with their work.

Circumstances in a lot of cases made it very profitable if not necessary for stretcher bearers to use German prisoners in transporting the wounded from the battlefield to the point where they were sent out in ambulances. In the incident I record here, the prisoners I had serving under me were young, probably between eighteen and twenty-one. They were intelligent and in good physical shape and I judged them to be decent, friendly and good chaps. They were not the hard-boiled, superior type German you sometimes read about; neither were they in the class that had to be chained to their machine gun. In fact, I never met any that was in that class. One of my buddies could speak their language and under the influence of our kind treatment they talked freely of the war and why they were fighting. They were tired of it, but like us with our Viet Nam little war they just couldn't figure a way to get out. A nation's war might be compared to quicksand; the harder one struggles the deeper he sinks and if it's a very big puddle he is in, one really needs help to get out and the more pride and the bigger the nation the harder it is to get out of the mess. There is no such thing as a clean muck hole or war. They both stink and the people that go to war carry the odor for a long time. It just won't go away.

The prisoners had heard that some Americans were bloodthirsty brutes. They realized that I was not like that, and that as long as they were under my care, I would protect them. They followed me as closely as a young pup follows its master and obeyed my orders as they would have their own colonel. Needless to say, we made an efficient team in getting out our wounded.

On one occasion, we were stopped for a short rest, and from the food we had gathered from discarded packs were satisfying our hunger when along came a lieutenant, so fresh from the States that the original shine from his newly purchased boots glistened in the sunlight. His military manners were that of a peacetime barrack officer. He had none of that human, natural tough manner that an officer picks up on the battlefield. His fancy tailor-made uniform, his perfect, sissified neatness, his shining buttons and official strut were as out of place at the front as my dirty garb would have been in a fancy military ballroom. That military dude came to this dirty, bearded, uniform-torn, rugged, grim-faced, battle weary, blood spattered field soldier and in an artificial, perhaps practiced gesture, and over-emphasized words of command said, "Who is in charge of these prisoners ?"

I slowly got to my feet, let my eyes roam from his fancy boots to the top of his head and then came to rest on his nice gold bar and said, "Sir, I am."

Then the lieutenant: "Where are your arms?"

My reply was, "Sir, in this war Red Cross men do not wear arms."

Then came the order, "You take those prisoners and turn them over to someone that can guard them."

I sometimes wonder what a predicament the lieutenant would have been in if I had said, "Here, lieutenant, you take 'em, you carry them back to the rear," and walked off and left him. The lieutenant was unarmed and evidently thought them dangerous and would have been afraid of them attacking him. He would have walked them all of three miles back to a prison depot, and when he was questioned about where he found them and told the men in charge that he took them away from a stretcher-bearer he in all probability would have been balled-out by some hard-boiled sergeant. Instead, I answered him in a voice that let him know that I meant it and no fooling.

"Sir, I am not taking orders from you today."

Well, so far as I know that ended the matter. He may have tried to report me, but if he did I never heard of it.

I don't want you to get the idea that I was a great guy or a sort of hell on wheels; I was neither. I am trying to portray me and the average soldier, how they felt and how they acted, why, and what it was like, the little things that happen in a big battle. For sure there were soldiers who are mean, talked and acted mean; but that type of soldier is in the minority in the army just as he is in civilian life. Another thing, the big mouthers are not always the best lawyers

140

or fighters. A sergeant's stripes, an officer's bar, eagle or star and a civilian's badge or shield should be evidence of authority and be given proper respect. On the other hand, they shouldn't step out of line and assume power that legally does not belong to them. People who possess these marks of rank should be made aware of the fact that it takes knowledge, character and personality along with rank to get the respect and authority that traditionally goes with it.

Chapter 16

We were troops in transit, paused and waiting for the final jump off at the enemy wherever needed. We were next in line for a try at the enemy. Like checkers, the master hand that guided our movements would send us to the right or left to check or block a German's move, or on a straight frontal attack as the play or military strategy demanded.

We were experienced line soldiers there were no bath houses or man-made showers where we spent our days and weeks. Water was a scarce item with too little to satisfy our thirst. There were occasions when one would go several days with none to wash his hands and would use clean dirt or sand to scour his mess kit. An all-over bath was a luxury that came at long intervals.

We were on the steep hillside because we were safe there. The meadow below could be dangerous, because any number of the enemy's shells could be aimed at the place, dropped and exploded down there. The height of our hill was between us and the Germans and while on the hillside it was practically impossible to drop a shell on us, but shells aimed just over the hill would land in the meadow. But water, nice, clean, clear, sparkling running water that glistened from sunshine as it peacefully ran by clean sandbars and over slick rocks as it moved its way through the beautiful but forbidden meadow. Forbidden because back beyond the Germans' line high up in the air was a German observation balloon. Beneath this sausage-shaped gas bag hung a basket-like structure in which rode a German with a long-range telescope and whose business was to spot targets for his artillery to shoot at. There was a good chance that he had spotted us and was sitting there waiting for the water-hungry Yanks to yield to the temptation and a large number of them go down there for a bath. The small stream had no banks, that is to say hardly any, certainly not enough to offer any protection from exploding shells. There had not been any shells to explode down there and some of us reasoned that the Germans were just waiting and would hold their fire if only a few ventured down into the meadow. Perhaps the Germans figured that we were fresh American recruits and would let a few go down and bathe in peace as a bait to bring large groups of others down and then would come the slaughter. I was interested in other things, more timid and more cautious and took less chances than a lot of fellows, so did not at that time give any consideration or thought to risking my hide for the sake of a bath. In fact I had years previous developed a taste for panoramic scenic views from hillsides and my place on the upper part of the hill was an ideal location from which to enjoy myself. The sky was crystal clear and there appeared to be a three-quarter dome where its extremities met the earth and a wooded area in the distance. It was a magnificent view and I was fascinated with what I saw.

As my eyes roamed farther afield, still higher in the air, off to my left I spotted a French observation balloon. As I watched and speculated about the man who rode in his seat thousands of feet up there in the air, I wondered if his job was not the clearest, most pleasant one in the whole war. This line of thought was interrupted when my attention was drawn to puffs of partially colored smoke that blossomed out high in the dome of the sky. The smoke puffs were to the right and north of the balloon and increased rapidly and formed a circular pattern as they grew more numerous in the sky. I knew that these puffs were made by exploding anti-aircraft shells and that up there invisible to me was an enemy plane. As the puffs moved in the general direction of the balloon, I realized that the balloon was the plane's target and if successful in getting through the barrage of bursting shells it would dive on the balloon and give it a burst of machine gun fire. The plane's incendiary bullets would set the balloon on fire and it would burst into a mass of flames and burn its way to earth.

This was a critical time, a race with life and death at stake. The anti-aircraft's exploding shells were literally forming a sheet of metal, a curtain of deadly fire that should block the plane's path that led to the balloon. The plane had a destructive mission to perform, the ground gunners had their duties and obligations. The balloon and the life of the observer were their job to protect and save. It was a human duel, a battle for life. Who would win? There had been cases when both the plane and the balloon with their human occupants came down in fiery flames. Such tragedies I do not like to witness. But this tragedy I must see. My eyes were turned to and focused on the balloon for there lay the battle's climax, death or victory for the balloon's crew.

Time, in a tragedy, moves slowly in the presence of scenes like this one. The observed had bailed out of his basket and his parachute is floating him down slowly, Oh! how slowly. Can he reach the earth before the plane can reach him with those machine gun bullets? The shells around the plane burst faster, the plane's speed toward the balloon appears slowed down, the French balloon observer has landed and is safe. The plane is still up there, but the odds are now against it making a strike for the balloon's ground crew in panic haste has pulled the balloon to earth and it appears that the plane has lost its target and as we see the exploding puffs move farther away from the area we know that the battle is over. The German plane will soon be heading for the Fatherland. And the balloon pretty soon will be back in the sky.

While I was watching the balloon drama, which was visible only to those of us who were on the higher part of the hill, some of the soldiers, the bolder of the water-tempted ones, had ventured out into the dangerous meadow and were stripped to the skin. As these early arrivals began soaping their bodies it began to appear to the rest of the men that the German artillery had more important business that day than chasing men from their bath.

Anyway, more and more men joined them, probably two hundred in all. Some of them were making a good use of the first opportunity they had had in many days to shave their long, coarse beards. Some others were washing their body-lice-infected clothes. There were as to be expected a lot of horse-play; jokes and laughter were in order and all seemed to be as happy as a bunch of kids who had just discovered a new community swimming pool. Soldiers just don't tolerate gloom and kill-joy attitudes in their lives.

The hillside and audience reminded one of a football stadium, though it was much longer, higher and the meadow was much larger than a football playing field, and the men in the audience had movement, freedom and space. There were no prepared seats or cover over any parts of it. Some of the men were writing letters to mother, wife or sweetheart, playing blackjack, shooting dice or just loitering around. I have no knowledge of the number or what organizations they belonged to but do know that there were both Marines and army infantrymen there.

There was no alcohol in that crowd; their spirits were not shackled by common men's restraints; they were natural free men, it was like a recess at school or young people in a holiday mood. They were rough men, tough men, and men who did not practice restraint in their language or jokes. They were having their break from a life of seriousness. They were happy to be alive and in a mood to enjoy themselves, and the men strung along the meadow branch had attracted their attention. The bathers had put themselves in a wide-open position that invited the roughnecks to attack them with what a civilian would resent as personal insults. The people in the meadow had of their own choosing become isolated actors and the butt of the audience's jokes and fun; their personal dignity had become public property to amuse or be abused by an uncouth, liberty-taking public mob who made their own rules of conduct as they went along. The bathers didn't appear to mind their role. The timid and really dignified had for the time lost their dignity or it just wasn't out there in the first place. They were among their own kind, roughnecks. Their ridicule and uninhibited uncouth comments were as free of restraint as their naked bodies.

The actors along the stream had quickly caught the spirit as well as the eyes of the crowd and the part they were to play in putting on a comedy show for an audience of several thousand men. They deliberately imparted an exaggerated version of a natural, amusing sight. Each gave his own interpretation of the act of undressing before a big audience. It was their version of a strip-tickle affair, the man's funny bone and not his romantic emotions were the object of their performance. Standing and getting a muddy foot into clean shorts require some skill. It was a mixture of the real and the unreal, some slipped and unintentionally flopped down on their butts. These slip-ups got the loudest laughs.

All but the most serious minded had momentarily forgotten that the eyes of Germany were upon them, and His Majesty the Kaiser's balloon artillery spotter was also watching the show and probably figuring when the cue for the shell to enter the scene be given.

Anyway, close to and just over the hill top there came the whizzing bark of a fast-falling shell to land with a bang. The earth trembled, hot metal dirt and pieces of rock spewed up and outward leaving a cone-shaped hole in the peaceful meadow. At the instant the noise of the approaching shell reached the ears of the experienced shell-dodgers, they hit the ground and by the time rock and dirt that had been flung upward and outward had returned to earth the two hundred bathers had crawled to their feet and made a dash for their clothes. No one was hurt. The audience roared with laughter. It sure enough was a comical scene and it took no exaggeration of the natural common acts to make it about the funniest thing one could want to see. Two hundred naked men with seconds, they thought, to grab up their garments and be gone from there. Two hundred men trying to get into their own and not some neighbor's clothes knowing full well that in all probability another shell was on its way.

The expected second shell was slow in coming. The mixed up, scrambled entanglements of arms, legs, shoes and other garments was slowly righting itself. Drawers, shoes and other personal apparel were matching up with their rightful owner. Most of the bathers had had enough. They dressed and half-dressed, finishing their job of dressing as they hopped and hobbled along, some with only one foot in a shoe. These had to face a jeering audience who accused them of being quitters, cowards and a bunch of sissies.

Those more optimistic in believing that no more shells were coming elected to remain a while longer and were made heroes by their audience, one in particular who had shaved one-half of his heavy black bearded face. Gosh! it would have taken more nerve to face the yelling mob with that face than to stay on and risk another shell. Having found his mirror, soap and razor, washed the dirt away and gotten all set to start shaving the other side of his face he turned and faced his audience and made them a dignified graceful bow. Well, there was no roof to raise but the roar that went up from his audience could have done just that. He and the others remaining at the branch were soon settled down as if their task had not been interrupted. But not for long, for the Germans were not through with their part in the show.

Many of those remaining had hugged the dirty bare earth at the coming of the first shell and were wading back into the stream and were busy washing the wet dirt and mud from their bodies when the warning buzz and shriek of another shell announced that the short period of wait was over and another shell was about to land in the meadow. As all good soldiers should, as the angry shell gave out its downward whisp those boys went down to earth a second time and again were too low to be hit by the small fragments that went flying from the exploded shell. This time there weren't so many, less surprise, and being better prepared for it there was less scrambling, and still nobody was hurt. A few, still naked, gathered up their clothes and lit out for the hillside. Others remained to finish dressing and were given a hand by their audience for their bravery in defying the Kaiser. The man shaving had not finished, stayed on until his job was finished, though two more shells landed in the meadow. On his way back he bowed right and left in recognition of the hand and cheers that greeted him.

The third act put on that day in our natural theater and stadium was a purely airplane show, and of such magnitude for that period in the early development of the warplane that the whole show seemed fantastic and unreal to us sitting there on the hillside. I had witnessed several planes brought down in flames by anti-aircraft fire, seen a two-plane dog fight and the remains of several more wrecked planes. I had had the experience of walking along, far removed from machine gun fire, when suddenly I woke to the realization that the dust kicked up at my feet was caused by a German airman shooting at me from a flying plane. I had lain shivering in my bunk as a German bomber roared over my head and dropped bombs on a nearby target.

But this incident and scene was something else. It rated a professional reporter's notice and the daily's headlines. It didn't make sense to me. I believe it unusual for World War I, maybe not for the second World War. The way it was fought, and the way both sides hightailed it back to their home bases indicated to me that the men on the two sides of the battle were surprised and shocked at the suddenness of their encounter in mass. Surely no two groups would choose to fight as they did. Perhaps both were on a hunting mission. But suppose one group could have maneuvered above and gotten on the tail of the other, say a thousand feet above. Holy Jupiter! I would've hated to have been the underdog in that kind of dog fight.

A hush of silence prevailed over the audience that only a few minutes previous were so noisy, gay and boisterous. Necks were

147

strained for a better view and all eyes were alerted to the new and different scene. Like a three-ring circus, one had to switch gaze from right to left because the actors in the dramatic airplane show at this stage of action were miles apart. Off to my left high in the cloudless sky were a large number of planes in a flying group formation traveling in a straight course at a steady, fast gait. We correctly judged them to be German planes.

At about the same distance away, off to my right, was another group of planes, equal in number, equally high in the air, and also coming rapidly toward us. These we judged to be Allied planes, probably Americans. We were awed and excited. It was a grand and unusual show for us to see, never before that near the front. We had mixed emotions of admiration, thrill and anticipated fear and shock. An enemy and our forces flying to meeting each other in a parade mass formation. From the straight course each group had lined up and was following, it appeared inevitable that there would be a head-on meeting and collision one or more thousand feet right out in front of where we were seated and an air battle of such magnitude would take place that history was in the making and it could be that we were to be a witness of the beginning of a new kind of war – a war in which land soldiers were replaced by air soldiers. Well, that was approximately fifty years ago and before the atom bomb was dreamed of.

From the speed of their approach and the narrowing of the distance between the two forces, our judgment that the battle would take place in our neighborhood was confirmed and our nervous tension was increased with the speed of their approach. As the slow tick of time moved on and the planes got nearer and nearer to us, we knew for a certainty that they would meet head-on in the air above our meadow, the stage of our hillside stadium. Our heartbeats grew louder and became regular thump, thumps in our throats. As the excitement ruled over the usual noisy crowd. Our eyes became a fixed stare, glued to the point of contact and meeting place of the opposing air forces.

They came straight on and out in front of our hill, probably seven hundred or fewer feet straight out and a couple of thousand or more feet higher than my seat on the hillside, then CAME TOGETHER.

There was no circling or maneuvering for position. It was as if there had been a fighting ring out there in space and all the fighters of the two sides moved straight into it. The fighting arena appeared over-crowded and too small to care for the large number of combatants that crowded into the small space. They were so crowded and things were happening so fast that my untrained eyes could not watch the acts of the individual planes as they came together. As I saw it, the two fighting groups became as one. I could not distinguish friend from foe. This scrambled mass of planes lasted maybe minutes. There must have been near lightning-like speed movements. As suddenly as the mix-up had brought them into the fighting arena, the entanglement dissolved and the opposite sides pulled out, reformed and headed back in the directions from which they came.

I saw one plane burst into flames and go diving off behind a nearby hill. There could have been others to suffer the same fate for I don't pretend to have been able to see the whole show, the thing was too big for that and the movements were too fast for me to have kept track of all of it.

Then, too, my attention was caught on a horrible scene that for the time blacked out all other parts of the show, a man floating out there in space. It was an aviator, a human body detached from plane or parachute, apparently alive, floating through the air. He was so near and the scene so clear and the view so plain that the movements of his body were clocked in my consciousness and my eyes followed the minute turns and twists of his body as it moved through space. These movements were visible and distinct for one-half of his three-thousand-foot journey to earth. At one time his legs spread apart and with his body's trunk formed a perfect letter Y, part of the time upside down. I can close my eyes now and see him as he was on that day forty-eight years ago. The emotional shock has stayed with me through all these many years and my emotional response is still so strong that it makes me uncomfortable to write of this event and these exceptional hours I experienced during World War One.

149

Chapter 17

The part my division and company took in the Saint-Mihiel drive was of special interest to me and it was the kind of battle I enjoy writing about. Like most old soldiers, I prefer to forget the horrors of war but feel that anyone who writes war stories should include enough of the worst features of war to cause his readers to have a distaste for it.

We had prepared for three thousand or more casualties, there were one thousand. I had wondered if there would be enough German prisoners turned over to me to make the carrying of our wounded back done quickly and efficiently. There proved to be more than enough. In fact there were more than three prisoners to each one of our wounded. While war and its battles are almost synonymous with hardship, I suffered comparatively no hardship during the battle of Saint-Mihiel. I did pull one stunt that made me shake with horror every time I thought of it for a week. It happened like this. Late on the night of the fifteenth, I went into a dark patch of woods, found an old shell hole that had a lot of rubbish in it. I pushed the rubbish around in the dark and made me a fairly comfortable place to lie down in and sleep. The next morning before daylight I was awakened by a loud roar to learn that my wooded camp that night had contained a number of French tanks and had to hustle out of my hole and dodge a coming tank which was, of course, moving without lights and the tank man had no idea that I was there. And when I went back to my shallow hole, and it was light enough for me to see, I found that the rubbish I had pushed around the night before among other things consisted of some old rusty discarded hand grenades. Frankly, a bed of snakes would have been preferable to those old grenades as a bed-fellow, and a herd of elephant preferable to those tanks for company.

Though we were expected to take two days to reach our assigned objective in the Saint-Mihiel drive, our boys completed their allotted task in one day. We found that contrary to expectations the battle was an easy one and proved to be a soldier's delight.

On this battlefield for the first time I saw a two-star general and several members of his personal staff riding horses considerably forward from the jumping off place only a few hours after the place had been mopped up by our forces.

Going up to our place on the line on the early morning before daybreak of September 15th was different, but not very much so, from similar trips made to battle fronts on the same mission of going over the top. This was to be a big show, a major battle, a significant one. For one thing General Pershing was in charge of it. Marines and doughboys were the chief actors. For the first time, General Pershing had been given an opportunity to prove himself a capable fighting general. He had under him for this battle better than four hundred thousand men. Success on this occasion meant prestige for the general and the American officers, as well as for the men under them. It could and did mean that the war would come to an end in the year 1918. Failure would have meant loss of prestige by the general and the shifting of more American soldiers back under the command of French and English generals and possibly the end of the general's career in France and World War One.

Without other victories this battle could not have been fought and yet from General Pershing's standpoint and the American soldier's welfare and prestige this easy won battle was possibly the most significant battle of World War One.

On our way to our company's place on the line, we passed by battery after battery of artillery of small and large guns, all pumping shell after shell at the Germans. Our scheduled place on the line was ideal for a grandstand view of the starting point of our drive in our sector of the front. We received only a token response to our own mass artillery fire, which helped to make it the most thrilling and magnificent display of artillery fire I had ever witnessed.

In this advance, our men were formed in lines a few spaces between the men in the line and some twenty to thirty yards between first and second lines. The many lines are referred to as waves. I do not recall trying to count the number of waves that struck out across the large field in front of where I was standing waiting my part of my company (that I was to trail) to take off following the other waves. There were probably fifteen waves and a number of them would be in my sight for a thousand yards and my view to the right and left extended many hundred yards. It was by ten-fold the largest number of men I had ever been able to see at one time and watch advancing on any battlefield in France. While I did not know at the time, this location had been chosen as the place at which a movie camera was set up and this wonderful panoramic view and the beginning of the battle of Saint-Mihiel was taken from a position just back of where my company joined the advancing lines.

My company was one of the last waves to take off. My position was a few yards back of my platoon and on the slightly elevated terrain where we led off, which gave me an ideal bird's-eye view of the show. I was so thrilled at the scene that it stamped an almost perfect detailed vision on my memory and years later when I saw a picture of the scene flashed on the screen in a movie theater, I immediately recognized it and as the picture continued saw myself in it going to the aid of a wounded soldier.

The question is often raised, "Just what do soldiers in the follow-up waves in an advancing line like ours do? What are their thoughts? Do they talk and what about?" These are natural questions, for as anyone could guess, one might follow along for hours and walk miles without personally coming in contact with the enemy. Frankly, they talk very little and when they do it is about something that has to do about their immediate surroundings. At the beginning I was interested in watching the whole show, but quickly my mind was taken up with my job of looking after wounded soldiers. Back lines are there to join forward lines when needed, and to take care of any of the enemy overlooked or left behind. They do the mopping up for the forward lines as they proceed on toward their objective. They fill in the losses, guard the flanks, take care of any enemy pockets left by the first lines as well as pick up and care for prisoners.

Most individuals in the ranks just walk forward until something happens that requires their attention and they get going working at the job of their assignment. Only officers and the noncoms know the location of their final objective and it is up to them to keep their lines headed in the right direction and their men properly distributed with reference to other outfits on their flanks. If an adjoining force, as often happened when we were flanked by French soldiers, peters out, the support lines are available to take their place and save their flanks. My job and the fellows with me was to carry back the wounded. My first obligation was to men of my own company but any wounded man, including the enemy, was served by me when my service was needed, and others were not available to serve them.

Just as one can drive a car along slowly and at the same time admire the scenery, so could we in the back wave talk and watch the scenery while advancing toward the enemy in open country. When we came to woods and other places where the enemy might be concealed every man should stay on the alert. Like walking through a south Georgia swamp no one should walk along unconcerned about what he hears or sees. Danger is not limited to the first wave; a sharpshooter may be hid out some where along your path, a shell may be coming your way, so your ears and eyes should stay open and your reflex nerves be ready to go into action at the instant a danger presents itself.

This is "it." The tide has changed. Now we can in truth say the promise we earlier made that, "The Yanks are coming," is an accomplished fact. "Mr. Lafayette, the Yanks are here." The Germans are on the run and a dream of the recent past of a complete victory and peace are in the process of becoming an accomplished achievement and goal. Just two short months more of harsh fighting and death-yielding tragedies and victory will be ours.

That day I could see with my own eyes a great army on the march and feel the swell of my own bosom with pride for my country. The delight of being one of its soldiers, and honored to be a member of the Race Horse Division, a member of the Devil Dog Marine Club and have the privilege to wear the globe, anchor and eagle, emblems of the Marine Corps. What more should I want? What further reward was needed? None! I say none! A chow hand, a private in the ranks and a first aid man. I am happy, I am satisfied, I am proud of the part I played and envy no man his medals or rank. My cup runneth over.

Getting back to the starting point and the beginning of the Saint-Mihiel drive, we see that the waiting period is over. In the distance we see the first wave is approaching the height of the ridge and my own platoon is swinging back into line and I take my place far enough back to keep the whole of the platoon under observation. We are off. We, our share of a four hundred thousand soldiers army, are stepping into battle.

153

We had gone let's say three hundred yards when I saw one of our men, a victim of a shrapnel slug, stagger and fall. He was one of our company's sergeants. We rushed to him and found that the slug had gone through his throat and blood was oozing out of the two holes from the left and right sides as he breathed. Death seemed imminent. He was still conscious but had no use of his muscles and, of course, could not speak. I did not think he could live more than a few seconds and eased him into a comfortable position. Then seeing that his breathing continued, I changed my mind, doubted his dying right away and we put him on our stretcher and hurriedly got him to the newly set-up first aid station a few hundred yards away in a shed. Ambulances had already begun to arrive and other stretcher-bearers were bringing in their wounded to the station, and the attendants at the place were loading them as fast as the ambulances could get in place to receive them. I motioned one of the attendants to come over to us. He took a hasty look, shook his head, and as good as said, "Let him die there where he is." By this time I had different ideas, so motioned my buddy. We got all set and when the next ambulance backed in place we rushed our man into it. My action was a little out of order, but what of it? The sergeant had a fighting chance, he was from my company and the attendant had no preference. It was a matter of judgment. The attendant thought the sergeant would die any minute and I felt differently. I feel pretty sure that the attendant was relieved rather than angry toward me. Naturally, it just wouldn't do to let thirty or more stretcher-bearers load their own wounded men when there were not room for all the patients to be loaded immediately on arrival to the station. Some needed to be rushed, some didn't. The dead would be taken care of after the rush was over. I knew the importance of leaving the loading to the attendants and this is the only case I didn't leave my patient in their hands.

A couple of months later while I was in the Marine paymaster's office in Paris, whom should I meet but this same sergeant. He had lived not only long enough to get to a well-equipped hospital but in all probability would live the normal three score ten average allotted time. He had lost the power of speech but in other respects appeared normal. The two scars were there showing where he got his and how close he came to meeting his death in the easy battle of the

Saint-Mihiel Drive. The impossible does happen. Wouldn't it be something if the fellow reads this, goes to his local movie house on the date of the fiftieth anniversary of the battle of Saint-Mihiel Drive and sees himself carried from the battlefield!

Now a word about gas masks, which were probably hated more than the poison gas which was used for the first time in our war and not much since. Poison gas was one of the main topics of conversation of our war and deserves a place in my story. Our American gas masks were big, and a clumsy nuisance to carry, and downright disagreeable and obnoxious to wear.

I was following a path through some woods one day and saw lying in the path thirty feet in front of me a cracked, opened shell from which was coming a white vapor. I stopped, saw that it was a gas shell. I did not put on my gas mask. Instead I tested to see from which direction a slight breeze was coming and detoured around the gas shell on the windward side and went on my way. I was, of course, alerted and was on the look out for more shells but didn't see any evidence of another shell.

On another occasion I had a wounded soldier to carry back to the first aid station and removed my gas mask, intending to replace it, but for some reason forgot to do so. We were in an open meadow and the Germans started dropping gas shells, fortunately behind us. I naturally speeded up our walk, the shells kept coming and were getting closer. I kept going faster and the shells moved as if we had been spotted and were aimed at us. We had a lead on them and never lost it and were almost at a fast dog trot before we were out of the meadow and free from danger of the gas. The fellow on the stretcher knew that they were gas shells and was as anxious as I to get away from them, so did not grumble any for the jolting he was getting. Most wounded men were in a hurry to get to a first aid station and on to a hospital. If they were conscious and not in an awful lot of pain or wounded in a vital part of their body the wounded person began speculating on the nice time he would have in the hospital. Very few complained about their wounds. All in time expected to return to their old outfit. And I think it important to return soldiers to their old companies.

The luckiest fellows are the ones that get wounded. A story is told of one lucky fellow that was wounded three times without ever actually being on the firing line. This fellow was wounded on the way up to the front line, sent back to a hospital, treated, sent back, but again was wounded before reaching the battle front. This is supposed to have happened three times and the war was ended before he was able to reach a fighting front. Whether it happened that way or not, the fact that the story was told as a good luck story seems to indicate how the men felt about being wounded. As a lot of us put it, our wound was our pass or ticket to a hospital, a clean sheet, liberty and maybe a trip to Paris. I was luckier than most of them – an ear and arm wound. I reached Paris just at the right time to get the most out of my ticket there.

Next to hospitals and liberty in some large city we experienced soldiers had dreams of serving in rest areas or "bon sectors." A bon sector, sometimes called a quiet sector, was where there was a kind of unspoken, understood truce where neither side bothered to fire on others and where both sides sent their overworked, tired soldiers for rest. Some were quieter and more peaceable and more desirable than others. At the time we moved into one of these places, we were let known that our orders were not to fire on the Germans unless fired upon. In this one we bathed and bombed for fish in a stream that ran between the lines. I was on the chow detail at the time. Two or three of the boys loaded up with hand grenades and went exploding the grenades in the deeper water upstream while others of us lined up downstream in shallow water and as the dead fish floated by we gathered them up. On one trip we caught enough fish for a fish fry supper for the company of two hundred and fifty men. I remember on one occasion there were crowds of soldiers all along the stream washing, bathing and just loitering. This unusually large number must have aroused the suspicion of the Germans for an observation plane came over and flying rather low flew up and down the stream and kept watch on us until he was convinced that we were unarmed and were not up to some devilment. On nights the Germans would put on old time dances, with lights blazing, and with the dance "calls" and music that drifted over to our side. On our side it was the usual card games and beer parties with male songs, shouts and laughter. At night their bombers would pass over, ignoring our lights and go on farther inland to find and bomb targets to the south of us. I was bunked down in a brick paper mill. I had doubted that a rifle bullet would go through a sheet of steel. My findings were that the power of the bullet knocked a plug out of the steel plate some larger than the size of the bullet. Next I tried shooting sparrows with the high-powered rifle. Well, with a direct hit the bird just disintegrated and all that was left was a bunch of feathers. After putting a few shots into the brick wall I decided I had rather have a brick wall than a sheet of steel for protection from a high powered bullet.

As was bound to happen, we next were headed for an entirely different kind of front. There would be nothing "bon" (good) about the front we were headed for. We began to meet ambulances returning from the front with men in them with their eyes covered and other bandages that indicated that they were gas casualties. I was traveling toward a gas-infested area.

Chapter 18

Pretty soon I will be writing what to you may be an unbelievable, strange story. My only defense is I can only write it as my memory dictates.

My day of departure from the Race Horse Division and The Devil Dogs Fighting Marine Brigade was celebrated by another magnificent achievement and victory. I have a few other small trinkets of merit received but consider my battle scar to be a badge of honor of which I am proud and offer it as evidence that I am entitled to share in the honor received by the Marine Brigade in the Belleau Wood and the whole of the Second Army Division on October 3-4, 1918.

It was on the night of the second of October that we went into a trench full of French soldiers who had tried and failed to take the ridge our trench was facing. There were dead in the trench which bore witness to the fact that it was a tough assignment and that the French had tried hard but just couldn't make the grade, and now in our sector it was my company and my battalion that had taken over the unfinished job of taking Mont Blanche Heights.

These heights had been in the hands of the Germans for almost four years for the simple reason that the French could not drive them out. It was a tough assignment, and one that had to be executed before we could get going with winning the war. As men and area goes, it was a small local battle that could well be ignored in the annals of history, yet especially to me it was the most important battle of the war. Its relation to other fronts made the taking of the heights an achievement that added to the distinction already won by the Marines and the Second Division. The immediate effect of the victory on other fronts made it one of the highlights of the whole war. Here I think it is in order for me to break my rule and quote others in my story.

"As a direct result of your victory, the German armies east and west of Rheims are in full retreat, and by drawing on yourselves several German divisions from other parts of the front you greatly assisted the victorious advance of the Allied armies between Cambrai and St. Quentin. To be able to say when this war is finished,

'I belonged to the 2nd Division, I fought with it at the battle of Blanch Mont Ridge,' will be the highest honor that can come to any man." John A. Lejeune, Major General, United States Marine Corps, Commanding

Maybe I am a dunce for writing it; this old codger was thrilled while typing the above citation. It was in this battle that I won a legal pass to a Red Cross Field Hospital in Paris and my association with the Second Army Division came to an end.

We had been on the go since daybreak and it was past midnight and there was, so far as we knew, no further need for our services. We were tired and worn out; tomorrow would be another tough day. It was time for us to call it a day, bunk down and get some rest and sleep. There would be more fighting and more work to do with the coming of another day, and now was our only chance for rest. We were in a deep ravine or broad gully. It was about the safest place one could hope to find that near the German line. It certainly wouldn't be exactly safe to be wandering around in the dark hunting for another ditch or hole. On further investigation, we found that someone, to make it safe, had in the very bottom of the gully dug down another twelve or sixteen inches and scooped out a place wide and long enough for two men to lay stretched out at full length with all of their body below the level of the ditch's bottom.

This extra feature had made the place as near shell proof as one could hope to find and for a certainty left no doubt in our minds as to the advisability of us bunking down there for the rest of the night. All one did to bunk down on the front, was to lay down, relax, close his eyes and sleep would follow.

The bullets may continue to whistle over the top of the ditch, small shells may whiz by and land a few yards away. The big ones high up in the skies may sing, whistle or moan as they pass on their flight to some distant target in the rear. The weary stretcher bearers would sleep through it until some change took place in the timing of the shells, or sometimes if it got very quiet on a noisy front the lack of noise would awaken a sleeping soldier. And it was rightly so, for lack of change was evidence that things were the same as when he lay down to sleep. Any change could be a warning that the Germans were getting ready to start something different, like the Germans

159

sending out a night patrol. On the other hand, if the shells began coming over faster, chattering of the machine guns are increased and especially if the sharp crack of the Springfield rifles begin to pop lively along the line, one would suspect that the Germans could be putting on an attack and it was time we were awake and alerted for trouble. But these things did not come to pass that night and we slept on through the night. That is until not long after four o'clock in the early morning of a new day.

It was not unusual, in fact a common practice, to make early morning attacks, so both sides apparently sent over more shells and there was a greater clatter of machine gun fire at this time of day. In case of attack, however, the artillery fire was more intense and there was more firing all along the whole front. After a time one began to feel that he could tell very well what was taking place along the fighting line by listening to the noise made by the different weapons and the intensity of their firing. Fortunately for us, there was only a small amount of change, not enough to disturb us, so we remained lying flat on our backs in the scooped out place in the gully and were thus protected when a shell came over and landed in our gully. The shell landed not more than two yards from the back of my head and a little to the right of our scooped out place. Only my right arm was above the level of the bottom of the ditch; evidently it was in a raised position which put it in the path of the parts of the exploded shell. A hot fragment from it went through my forearm, not stopping in the arm or blouse sleeve.

It was more like a fierce, hard, jarring blow than being pierced by a sharp edged object. Instead of being knocked unconscious, I was literally knocked to my feet. I was never before aroused so quickly and so completely from sleep and to awareness of my surroundings than on that occasion. And a distinct memory of the shell hole, my buddy and my surroundings still linger in my memory. I was dancing around as you have seen some child do on stumping his big toe against a rock. I could not stand still, get back into the hole or lie down. One of the main muscle tenders had been severed and the arm fell to my side and just hung there and felt like it weighed a ton. A rough, splintery scrap of hot iron had plowed its way through my arm cutting, but mostly tearing its way through, leaving ragged, scorched, torn nerves, flesh and muscles in its path. I had no use of

160

arm, hand or fingers. My arm was just hanging there. I would lift it up with my left hand and pull it across my breast, but no position seemed to be the right one. Added to this was that dead-like feeling one's arm has when the circulation is cut off. The sense of touch had left my arm, hand and fingers, but a continuous ache stayed with me. There was scarcely any bleeding; the hot iron slug had taken care of that. My head had received a jar from the near explosion and there was a small amount of blood in my right ear and for the time I was practically deaf in both ears. Over the years my inner ear trouble has given me more trouble than my deafness and the arm. One can more easily understand and adjust himself to the aches and weakness of an injured arm and deafness than to the strange and unpredictable action of inner ear nerves.

Even though a lot of shells were falling outside our ditch making it dangerous to leave the protection provided by it and I actually knew that there was no emergency reason for hurrying out, my misery would not permit me to listen to reason. I had to get going, nothing else would do. No, my companion was not hurt. I was nearer the exploded shell than he, and he was wholly below the earth's surface, while my arm was above the surface and in the path of the flying fragments from need for physical aid. Under such circumstances the wounded men were supposed to make it back alone and a stretcher-bearer was supposed to remain at the front and be available to serve those that needed his help. He did not go back with me because with all the shooting going on and the many shells exploding in the area it was certain to result in casualties that would need him badly.

As for giving out or fainting, tough soldiers were denied that luxury. As for being lonely, my misery was plenty company and a guarantee that I would not sit down on the way out and go to sleep.

All I remember about the trip was that I had a hard time carrying that right arm of mine. The muscles not damaged in the arm also refused to function. The cut nerves that led to my hand and fingers registered pain and ache in both hand and fingers; possibly it was the scorched flesh, nerves and muscles rather than the ragged cut that was causing the pain. I am sure a freely bleeding wound would not hurt as my arm did. I made it after a time, my first stop on a long trail to a hospital in. Paris. A story that calls for a chapter of its own.

Chapter 19

The first aid station was set up alongside a main road in a deep roadside dugout. I don't recall how far it was from the front or how long it took to make it to the station. I arrived none the worse for the trip and by the time I got there it was good daylight, and some other walking casualties were also there. Since it was a warm, pleasant morning and no shells were falling in that area, everybody had moved out into the open, in the space between the dugout and the road. The dugout was close to ten or fifteen feet deep with a long set of dug steps leading to its bottom. A nice place to be while shells were falling, but otherwise the open air, uncovered front was a more pleasant place to be.

The medical corpsman gave me the accustomed tetanus shot and after bandaging my arm and giving me some dope to ease my pain, he suggested that I go into the dugout and lie down. One look at the long row of steps leading down to the bottom of it, I shook my head and said, "I want to get going to a hospital." The attendant smiled and said, "Who doesn't?" and moved on to another patient.

I moved over close to the road and in a little while an empty truck headed toward the rear came up and I thumbed a ride. The dope had not so far had much effect on stopping my pain and the arm seemed to be enlarging and was growing heavier all the time. I was still restless and had a job adjusting myself to the truck's seat. As for thoughts, I had none, I was just moving along with the tide and fate, no plans, just an urge to get to a hospital and the comforts that others had described to me.

The driver knowing that I was wounded and in misery, was kind enough to make things as comfortable for me as he could. And when we drove into a small railroad town he left the main road and drove around to a tent field emergency hospital and put me out in front of one of the tents. I went up and glanced in the tent and saw doctors and nurses busy with some serious emergency cases. While by then I was beginning to feel the effects of the dope, I realized that mine was not an emergency case and that this was not the right hospital for me. I moved around and found an empty tent with the side flaps raised and which contained some army cots. My pains had begun to ease up a bit and I felt drowsy. I went in and lay down on one of the cots and soon fell into a troublesome dazed-like sleep.

For hours I lay there, part of the time in a kind of dazed condition of half consciousness and a dopey wakefulness. Most of the time I was not conscious of any pain, at others I would flounder around trying to adjust my body to the cot, never fully awake or fully aware of the passing of time, or conscious enough to want to get up and start going somewhere.

It was probably three o'clock in the afternoon when I saw a procession of people going by the open flap of my tent. In the lead were the serious cases carried on stretchers, and accompanied by nurses. Following these were walking casualties. Some seemed to be enjoying their walk. I was not fully aware of what it was all about but nevertheless I left my tent and started tailing along behind the procession. We came to a railroad track and standing there was a hospital train. I had sense enough to recognize it for what it was, though it was the first one I had ever seen. Being the tail end of the line, I was the last to go aboard the train and my car proved to be an old passenger coach, judging by the quality of the seats and other facilities, about third class is my guess. The seats were unpadded, springless, and wood constructed with wooden backs, seats and arms. I was still dopey but managed to get aboard and fortunately found an unoccupied seat and took it all to myself.

By this time my arm was swollen considerably and as the dope that had been given me in the early part of the day was becoming less effective in killing the pain it again began to show up in my arm and in no time I became very restless once again. It was not the kind of pain that makes some people cry out and others to moan. It was a continuous, aggravating misery, of uncomfortable, tiresome, weary, physically worn-out condition that holds one's mind focused on it without letup. It was like being weighted down with a heavy load, completely tired out without hope of relief. I was half conscious during the night and while I have no knowledge of it, it is possible that someone gave me some more dope. I suspect this because before morning my arm hurt less and I was more dopey than in the early part of the night.

I remember only two things about the trip, one was receiving a cup of warm chocolate along with sweet crackers, the other was my

163

almost endless struggle to find a comfortable way to rest in my seat. I have known people to roll and tumble in bed. I could neither roll or tumble. The seat was not wide or long enough for that.

The most miserable position was to let my arm hang down. The most comfortable one was for me to lay flat on my back with my feet sticking straight up in the air with my injured arm across my chest. But it wasn't satisfactory to let it stay in any position for more than a few minutes at a time. The length of the seat was just long enough to accommodate my head and trunk part of my body. There were too many people going up and down the coach's narrow aisle to let my feet and legs hang over the seat's arm out into the aisle. I know that it must have been one ridiculous looking way to occupy a passenger seat but it was the best I could do in my battle for a little comfort. Well, this struggle between the seat, my arm and comfort lasted a good twelve hours or more before the night of misery ended in a railroad station in the city of Paris, some time before daybreak on October 5th, 1918.

My dream, the dream of all the fighting soldiers in my outfit, had for me come true. I was again dopey and didn't realize fully where I had landed, and was not conscious enough to care. I found a whole seat a little apart from the others and showed promptly my appreciation of the padded seats by dozing off to sleep. When I came to myself most of the folks I had been following had left the station and the tail end of the remaining procession was going out the station door.

There were many hospitals in Paris, all the patients coming in on a train most certainly were not sent to the same hospital. Only the stretcher cases had attendants to look after them. No doubt all along the way somebody was making announcements and telling us what to do and where to go, but due to my deafness and inability to communicate with the others and a desire to be left alone I was not in a true sense one of the party. I was just tagging along. Where they went I followed, the tail end of a long line. I doubt that my name was on any roll, certainly I had not answered to any roll call or been questioned by any one. I was among those required to look out for himself. We had no nursemaids to look after us. I was not in communication with anyone; I was not in any mood for companionship, and no one tried to break in on my privacy. The few hospital workers along had their hands full to look after the helpless wounded, the rest of us were supposed to be able to take care of ourselves. It seems that from this station the procession was split up and the patients sent to the different hospitals.

Anyway, when I got outside the station I had no one to follow. My crowd was nowhere in sight. I was alone there at the station's side entrance. I was conscious enough to know that I was in a large city and guessed it to be Paris and having been left behind realized that it was up to me to find my own way to a hospital. I knew that the hospitals had names and numbers; the only name I could think of was Red Cross. So when I saw a horse-drawn cab, I crawled into it and probably yelled Red Cross Hospital. The taxi driver could see from my dirty fighting garb and bandage that I was wounded and just in from the front. Whether he understood English or not, he understood Red Cross Hospital, and the rest was self-evident, and needed no explaining. He just nodded and we were off in a trot. How far did we have to go, I haven't the least idea, I was too dopey to remember anything I saw on the route and probably slept all the way there.

What counted was that I was on my way to a hospital and I had heard that the Red Cross ones were preferable to those of the regular army. While I don't know about that even now, but not knowing I would guess it true and believe our nurses treated us more human and with greater consideration than would have professional army nurses, and in a lot of cases the same would apply to doctors. I don't see how I could have been treated better without becoming a spoiled patient. Their paternal care went beyond their technical duties.

I don't know whether I was due to pay the cab driver or not. I am sure I would have given him a few franks if I had thought of it. Frenchmen are not timid about asking for pay but few men right from the front have any money with them. Pay or no pay this was one American soldier few would have wanted to carry on an argument with at that time.

The hospital was inside the gate of a famous racetrack and that morning it looked like it contained hundreds of tents. (It really wasn't a very large hospital.) All the patients arriving that morning, that were on the same train as I, no doubt by the time I had arrived had been placed in some tent, but where? How was I to know or tell?

The cab driver put me out just inside the main gate. I was too dopey to do any clear thinking and had never been in any hospital in or out of the service and had not the least idea how one registered and was received into one. I was just standing there trying to decide which way to go when along came about twenty or thirty men (they turned out to be orderlies). I had by this time developed the habit of just following folks and trailed along with this procession. This gang led me into a mess hall and as I passed by the serving pots, some guy handed me a plate of beans, bacon, a hunk of bread and a cup of coffee. All I had had to eat the past thirty-six hours had been a few cups of warm chocolate and sweet crackers. I gobbled the food down and went outside. I was standing outside wondering what to do now, or where to go when a fast walking nurse came by. When I yelled at her, not realizing how deaf I was, the poor thing jumped, then saw the dirty bandage on my arm and realizing that I was a newly arrived patient started talking a whole rigmarole of words, the only one I caught was "x-ray." I yelled back at her, "Where is the x-ray?" She pointed her finger at a tent and was off as if she was trying to get gone from there before I had time to think up another question to yell at her. I went over to the tent she had pointed out, entered it but found no one there.

It was early and none of the attendants had shown up for work. I looked around, found a table, and realizing that I was sleepy crawled upon it and was immediately sound asleep. When I awoke a man was standing above me looking at me with a puzzled expression on his face. I pointed at my bandage and yelled "x-ray." He laughed and said, "O.K., soldier." And though he seemed amused about something he went on with his work and when he was through he filled out a tag and on the back wrote something and tied the tag to my arm. Then I asked, "Where do I go from here?" He faced me squarely and with his lips formed the words, "Operation next." I went outside and stood for a few minutes and another nurse came along, by this time probably the word was getting around about me. When I yelled at the nurse, "Where is the operation tent?" she didn't seem surprised or slacken her pace or speak, she just pointed toward another tent and was on her way. I entered the tent to find that none of the attendants had arrived there, either. As I was still sleepy, I found another table, crawled upon it, lay down and was soon asleep. I awakened this time to find several people around me and that's all I remember of what happened in that room, except I could have been there on the operation table dreaming it. Next, my memory moves to a deep hole or pool filled with some kind of thick slimy liquid and my head is beneath the surface and I am having a terrible time trying to keep from strangling on it.

After a blank period my memory picks up another vision I had. It appears that I had been asking what is hell like and the answer comes back, "this is it," as I experienced what hell is like. Well, I am not going to try to describe it, except that it has some of the features associated with the spin and whorl that associates itself with a severe attack of vertigo, with the added horror of the conviction that it would last throughout eternity. One of the main features of this hell was the complete loss of any hope that the punishment would ever end. Now I take pride in the thought that I am a practical man, and that there is a physical reason and proper explanation and answer to every mystery. Even so, for a number of years after the war, every time I had a severe attack of vertigo that continued very long, my thoughts moved back to my vision and my mind would say "this may be it," the one that will never end.

Now I am going to do a little guessing. First an ear specialist told me that he could trigger a case of vertigo by putting a fluid in the inner ear. Now my guess is that while I was under the influence of an anesthetic, I vomited up that plate of beans, which caused the first vision and that the doctors in cleaning out my injured ear triggered my first case of vertigo. But there was a third vision, that has stayed with me and its influence has helped to balance off the hurt to my emotions of the second one. In it I was floating in space, in the realms of absolute bliss, completely free of any pain or discomfort with complete faith that I was under the complete protection of Christ. These things are put in this manuscript because they have had a lot to do with my life, and though they were visionary incidents they have left their mark, influenced, handicapped and aided me as I have journeyed along through the past forty-odd years. It was one of the things the war did for me. I have experienced the complete loss of hope, I know what it is like. I have experienced complete faith, I know what it is like. The complete loss of hope is hell, the complete possession of faith is heaven.

The hearing in my right ear never improved very much, while that of my left ear was different. A lot of people have been temporarily deafened by loud explosions. The left ear was nearly back to normal when I regained consciousness. My hearing ability varies from time to time, apparently I hear best after having lain abed for a while.

Immediately after I recovered from my anesthetics, one of the boys wanted to know if I was from Georgia.

I told him I was. "Oh, boy! You slept too long," he said, and continued with the statement that a whole troop of pretty girls from Georgia a while back came through the ward inquiring if any of them were from that state. Now, wouldn't that have been something? For the lady leading that bunch of Georgia girls was none other than the wife of my congressman, from the small city of Newnan, and if she had met me she would have written my widowed mother and told her of visiting her son in a Red Cross Hospital in Paris. She was the kind of person that would have done just that. Not for publicity, but because she had a heart and mind that understood and felt for people.

The service men in the fast-moving fighting units in France had trouble getting paid; some and probably the majority of the wounded that were carried to the hospitals hadn't been paid in from two to three and four months. The wife of my congressman, the wife of the secretary of the navy and the wife of the Marine Corps commander were cronies and visited together in France. They learned about the Marines not being able to get paid, succeeded in getting it so that any Marine in one of the hospitals in Paris could go to the Marine's paymaster office and draw his back pay. Naturally, all of the army casualties were jealous of us. This explains how-come we Marines had money to spend in Paris. Some soldiers were so desperately in need of francs that they stole sheets, blankets and pillow slips from the hospitals and sold them on the black market. A lot of the much prized American candy and cigarettes also found its way into the hands of the French. Soldiers are taught to take what is necessary for their survival and there are some that stretch that word to include just about anything they want. And war spirit being what it is and our allies what they are, it ought to be understood that where U.S. soldiers are stationed there are going to be black markets.

The above information about the Marines' pay came to me from my congressman's wife in a friendly conversation. No colonel or two star general would have been given a more pleasant and gracious treatment than was awarded me, a buck private and common soldier in the ranks. She and her husband were the kind of people we like to have in Washington. They never took power for power's sake. They were people, understood people and considered it a pleasure and privilege to have an opportunity to serve. They were not ambitious climbers. They were not narrow-minded, modern moderates who are arrogant and over-burdened with self-righteousness and self-esteem.

Chapter 20

I was lying there feeling fine, so it did not occur to me to call an orderly when I felt the need to go to the bathroom. I eased out from my blanket, slid my feet to the floor and went through the usual process of standing on my feet and went sprawling on the floor. Only my dignity suffered any injury from the fall, but before I could even begin figuring out what had happened to me to take the starch out of my knees (the knee joints and muscles seemed as limber as a dishrag) the head nurse was there giving me a tongue lashing that left no doubt in my mind. I know now definitely that I was a bed patient and would remain one until she gave me permission to leave it. Bed patients were shown preference in many ways by the ward workers and the same was true of the visitors that dropped in to see us. It was ignorance and not an act of rebellion that caused this violation of the hospital's rules.

Our doctor left most of the dressing of our wounds dressing to our head nurse, and only occasionally checked the improvement and the healing after it was well started on the way to recovery. I quickly made friends with our nurses and aides. All of them rated A-1 in my estimation. They were good, prompt, friendly and efficient, and only once did I deserve and get a scolding.

On the second day the nurse gave me an opportunity to examine my arm. I found that the arm had swollen to three times its normal size. The doctor had gone into it and trimmed out all the ragged flesh and muscles and had left a big hole all the way through the arm from back to front. I could have actually run three fingers in the hole and two all the way through it. The dressing of it consisted of packing the hole full of gauze soaked in Dakin's solution. Each morning all the old gauze would be pulled out and the hole repacked with new. Where the gauze came in contact with the raw flesh, especially if it was too dry, it would stick to the flesh and the removing of it would be very painful. To keep my mind from concentrating on the arm and pain while the nurse was removing the old gauze from my wound I would start talking a blue streak. One of the aides caught on to what I was doing and cooperated with me and furnished me with an audience each time my arm was dressed.

In order to keep the gauze from becoming dry they inserted a glass tube into the arm and the Dakin's solution was pumped into the arm whenever a need for it was indicated. My arm healed rapidly but in a bent twisted position and my fingers were drawn and I didn't have use or sense of touch in them.

It was the doctor's idea to let it get very well on the road of healing and then, by exercising the arm and fingers, I could in time straighten the arm and regain the use of my fingers. It took time, in fact nearly four years, before my arm was completely straight and before my fingers were back near normal. I have never gotten where I can throw a rock or anything with force, neither can I reach over to my shoulder or to my back with my right hand to the extent I can with the left one. There were other weaknesses. The arm has a tendency to give out completely when used over a long period of time, even typing this. It is continuous use rather than heavy work that has this effect on it.

I just don't know how many patients we had in our ward, maybe thirty-five, probably more. We had a great variety of cases, all but a very few had suffered gunshot wounds. Three or four said that they had been gassed but did not show any outside evidence of it though it could have been that their lungs were in a very bad shape. We had a few that had lost a limb. One patient had lost an arm removed at the shoulder joint and a leg above his knee. When I was able to get out of my bed and walk around I sometimes visited with the others. There was no grumbling or self-pity among those that had suffered the greatest losses. They talked freely of their loss of limbs and joked about themselves and their loss. The more seriously wounded seemed to have the greatest ability to take their pain in silence.

My first real visitor was a French girl, probably in her twenties. She was a student in the University of Paris. She could speak more understandable English than some of the boys in the American uniform I had met. I was delighted with her and we seemed to have a mutual point of interest. She wanted to practice her English on me and perhaps get some grass roots knowledge of American people. I wanted to know about her college, the French people and, of course, thought of the advantage it would be for me to have an English-speaking French girl in the city.

She visited with me three times in one week, which suited me just fine. But for some reason, whether it was her motherly instinct to protect one of her boys from a sophisticated French woman, or that it was not good for us to have a regular lady friend, or it could be that there had developed jealousy on the part of my close bed neighbors who did not figure that I deserved special treatment, anyway some objection to her was expressed and she was let know that she was not welcome and stopped coming.

When I was well enough to get out and go places, while in Paris I met another French woman who could speak good English; in fact she could speak four modern languages. While the visiting French university student acted like a modern liberal college junior, this one was really sophisticated, a real internationalist who was equally at home in a half dozen countries of Europe. Really, she was way out of my class and though I appreciated the experience I was a little uncomfortable in her company. There was a tiny feeling on my part that I was being adopted as one of her pets, a role I was totally unsuited for. She was too sophisticated for my taste. The working French girls from poor families who knew no more English than I knew French (two years high school French) were a lot more fun than this too sophisticated English-speaking one. As you know, love has a language of its own and when two people are attracted toward each other the twinkle of an eye, the wrinkle of a frown and the lingering of a smile carry messages that are more informative and convincing than spoken words. Lack of words proved a big handicap in making future dates and in the planning of another meeting place but proved to be no barrier to making love. In fact, one of the most delightful little sweethearts of my younger days was a jolly cute little French maid who could speak only the French language and was not the least bit sophisticated, forward or bold. She was just a sweet kid, beautiful as a spring rose, fresh as a morning dew drop and as affectionate as an innocent sweet child. Unusual, some would say, of a French mademoiselle. I agree, she was an exception to the rule. But remember it is the exceptions and not the run of the mill that linger in the old man's memory.

Thinking and writing the above reminds me that one day the Red Cross doughnut truck drove into the hospital yard and behind the steering wheel sat the cutest ninety pound Red Cross worker I ever did see. In minutes the cripples and some not so crippled surrounded her truck and each was given one doughnut. I naturally was first in line and that little doughnut tasted so good! I wanted so much to get up close to that cute little number, so I dropped back into the doughnut line and in as pathetic a manner as I could master, with a sad pleading look and smile ever so humble, I reached with my bandaged arm in a pleading way for more. She from her seat in the truck bent over, ever so close, looked me in the eye, sorter pucked her smiling bewitching lips, and instead of handing me another doughnut, you know what? Of course, you don't. She said, "Piggy, piggy, piggy!"

Chapter 21

I was on a sightseeing tour of Paris guided by our Red Cross leader. We were visiting the tomb of Napoleon and there was a considerable number of French people present. Everything was moving along in a normal way when suddenly there seemed to be developing considerable excitement in the crowd that spread rapidly throughout the large hall and the people began to embrace each other, and to clap their hands. There were shouts and laughter filled with gleeful excitement. Some were laughing with tears running down their cheeks. Finally the word was passed to me that the war was over.

We had access to an English afternoon paper at the hospital. We wanted to believe the good news, yet refused to accept it as a fact until we could read it in our own language. We became anxious to get back to the hospital and read it in our papers. When our paper arrived we snatched it up and started searching the war news, only to be terribly disappointed. Not one single line of officially signed news was found that offered any authentic proof for the belief that the war was over. Only hints and speculations by civilian writers. We went to bed that night still hoping but in a kind of frustrated doubt. The morning papers added hope and convinced some that it would end at eleven o'clock that morning, but there were loopholes in the news that meant that circumstances could occur that might delay the cease-fire orders. We were almost convinced but would have to wait until the hour came before we could know for sure.

All our eyes watched and wondered as the clock's hands moved slowly toward the designated time; maybe our clock was fast. Eleven o'clock came and still no evidence that the war was over. I had gone outside and was standing facing the grandstand of the racetrack when a man stepped into view and in a loud voice began addressing a bunch of French carpenters who were working on the roofs of some buildings being constructed out in front of the stand. At the close of his few remarks, the carpenters threw their hammers into the air and let forth a loud yell and immediately following was the boom of an artillery gun which continued boom after boom. Now I had the evidence I had been waiting for. The celebration was on and the boom of the army's gun made it official. By our clock it was eleven minutes and a few seconds after eleven o'clock and, as I remember it, eleventh month, eleven seconds after the eleventh hour of the eleventh day of the year 1918.

I made my way back into the ward. All of us were hopeful and a little better than half-way expecting it. So we were not exactly surprised and some of the more optimistic boys had been making preparations and were ready to start celebrating. I never expect to see a happier bunch of people than the wounded in our ward. Someone had placed a big dish pan on the broad chest of our Texan patient, who had lost both an arm and leg. He had a long handled serving ladle in his good hand and was banging away on the pan. It was a never to be forgotten scene. Probably two-thirds of our ward's patients were confined to their beds and it was they that were shown preference and given the loudest noise makers that could be found and it was they that turned the ward into a jubilee house of happy celebrants. Smiles and laughter and many manifestations of excitement and joy filled the room. Their bosoms were overflowing with joy that spilt out into the air waves and was so impressive that there was a response in my own breast and my own emotions tingled with gladness for them, my own self was lost in a kind of community feeling. I was aroused by and for them rather than for something that had come to me. It was an unselfish joy and was made greater because it was free of limitations. A height of pure joy, rarely obtained by anyone. Thoughts of my own self were for the time eliminated, my compassion was for them. Their sacrifice was much greater than mine, had not been in vain; they had lived to see the fulfillment of their effort and prayer and to enjoy the fruits of their victory. They did not grumble about having paid a greater part of the cost of the war. They were thankful and overjoyed just to be alive and to live to this day, November the eleventh 1918.

The celebration in the city of Paris was something to see. An experience worth remembering and itself had a depth of compassion rarely experienced by people and I wouldn't have missed it for anything, though it did not reach the spiritual depth or the heart's overflowing personal compassion and bosom-filled excitement and depth in joy as did the small ward celebration in the Red Cross Hospital.

In my time, Paris was recognized as the play city of the recognized world. The French people were, and I suspect still are, the most enthusiastic public demonstrators of all people on earth. So every person that possibly could started for Paris and the celebration that all knew was already beginning and would reach its peak by nightfall. One member of our ward was wounded in his leg but could hobble along very well, and my arm was in an excellent healing condition and neither of us had let our wounds weaken us very much. As compared with most civilians we were still tough, everywhere except in our wounded limbs. We teamed up and applied for passes into Paris. Our good doctor complied with our request and immediately after an early supper we walked over to the station and boarded a subway train into the heart of the city.

The names of parks, squares, avenues and thoroughfares have skipped my memory, but the memory and images of the masses of people who crowded into the more popular section of Paris is still with me. An area that would measure close to one square mile was barred to all wheel traffic and turned into the gathering place for more than a million people where they could meet and together celebrate the end of the war. I did not see any babies or young children but everybody other than these seemed to be there. The young, middle-aged and old were in the crowd; soldiers and office clerks, factory workers and society dames, hospital patients and nurses, they were all there and in that whole mass of people I did not see a single drunk or any evidence that any police supervision was needed to keep the members of the crowd from disorderly conduct. The crowd was boisterous in a friendly way, free and happy and everything was done in a spirit of fun, it just didn't seem possible for tempers to flare up and hard feelings to develop in that happy crowd.

Apparently the old had lost their age, the mature their dignity, and reserve was overcome with enthusiasm. A magic wand had turned them all into a frolicking bunch of children. Restraint and personal discipline had evaporated into thin air as the black smoke disappeared from the last shot of an angry gun.

The people from their president down to the street sweepers, the prima donnas down to the factory working girls, they were all enthusiastic demonstrators of the art of osculation.

176

Even our pompous, dignified President Woodrow Wilson in Paris a short time later caught the fever and rode through the city throwing kisses at the yelling mob of Frenchmen, a strange sight I hadn't anticipated seeing.

Yes, it was a kissing crowd, a dancing crowd, a singing crowd, a war shackled people suddenly free from their bonds. A sad people made happy and whose deadened spirits had suddenly blossomed back to life by that magic word PEACE. It was a wonderful crowd, a wonderful celebration and it was great to be in "Gay Paree" on the night of November eleventh of the year 1918.

In my wildest dream I had never imagined that my trail along the rainbow's path would lead to such rewards as was mine on this night. I was never kissed so much in all the days of my life. Every wounded soldier was a hero, and every hero was rewarded and decorated over and again with a sweet kiss upon his brow and many times too numerous to count his lips shared in the honors.

Back in 1918, we still had a lot of stately, dignified, reserved matrons of the old school, who frowned upon a public display of affections of love between boy and girl. Lady-like modesty and gentleman-like conduct was expected of all respectable people. Only engaged couples and close relatives were suppose to kiss and then only in private.

Now many Frenchmen and especially French soldiers are proud of their many romantic conquests and take pride in their ability to practice their art, where others dare not tread, and are delighted to have an opportunity to demonstrate their skill. While most of us require a little cooperation on the part of the girls, these fellows seem to be able to go it alone.

During the heights of our fun, I happened to glance up and saw standing on a curbstone one of our American stately women. She was looking out over the crowd and her mind was as readable as an open book. She had an expression of frowning disgust written in every line of her face.

The poor soul, of course she didn't know it, but she was actually issuing a double dare to every old French-man in sight, "Come and kiss me if you dare." I said to myself "Wow, I want to see that." I wasn't long; I saw a French soldier, the proud owner of an extra long, curled at its two ends, pair of mustaches easing around to the matron's rear. He threw his arms over and around her shoulder and bent her backward until she fell in the folds of his arms with her face directly under his and kissed her squarely in her mouth, turned her loose and disappeared in the crowd. It was done so gracefully, so skillfully, and so quickly that the matron was no doubt shocked out of her wits and with sputtering indignation gathered up what dignity she had left and hastily made her way back to her hotel. You may rest assured that she never forgot that kiss. It was probably her most shocking experience with the male species. As she grew older she no doubt became fond of her own story and told of the episode to all of her grandnieces and old cronies.

The French people during the time I was staying in Paris were well disciplined; the policeman's orders were accepted and obeyed without question. No doubt, a time had been set and orders given and well advertised when the crowd should disperse and go home. My buddy and I didn't know about these things and hadn't given the matter a thought. We had no duties and time meant nothing to us. Without any hurly-burly or indicated reason the crowds just dissolved and disappeared. Only when the streets begin to take on a deserted look did we realize that the party was over and we started strolling in the direction of our subway station. It was probably three-quarters of a mile away. We were in no hurry. Why should we be? It was a good night to be out and there was no one that would be upset if we were a little late in getting in. It was a beautiful night. We didn't know the time, probably a little after twelve. It really made no difference to us, just so we got in before our head nurse came on duty for the new day. So we just strolled along the almost deserted streets. We finally arrived at our subway station to find the entrance barred by a policeman. After a lot of talk and arguing, we were convinced that the trains were finished. We knew we could not ride a train home that night. Now that's something of a mess for us to be in, two hospital patients stranded in Paris after midnight. We sat down on the curb outside the station and were discussing our plight when along came another American soldier who told us that he knew an English lady who would take us in for the night. So we struck out to find the English lady. She was a kind, pleasant grey-haired, cultured lady of let's say fifty-five. She expressed sympathy for us and said we would be perfectly welcome to sleep on the carpet of her living room floor and was sorry that she had nothing better to offer us. In the course of the conversation she had remarked that all her rooms were dated. That word "dated" stuck in my mind and I did a little snooping and by what I saw and making proper deductions I learned that the place was an English public house with girls kept for the entertainment of English soldiers.

After giving the idea a little thought, I discarded the thought of spending the night in Paris and began to mull over how we could find our way back to our hospital at that time of night. Our hospital was outside the old walls of Paris and on the right side of the river, thus by first finding the river and following it outside of the city wall and then turning squarely to the right we would surely come in sight of our hospital. How simple. But try following a river several miles through a large city! No, it wasn't as bad as I make it seem. It was a quiet and pleasant night, a delightful one for a stroll.

We arrived in sight of our hospital just at break of day and finally got into our ward while breakfast was being served. Many eyebrows were lifted, one of the aides teased me a bit, but no questions were asked and I am sure neither our head nurse or our doctor ever learned that we had been out all night. By getting new passes and keeping some of the old ones I was able to go into the city almost any time I wanted to make the trip.

I was in the city of Paris when President Wilson arrived for the peace conference and was eye witness to the parade of all the delegates and top leaders of the Allied nations and their armies.

My hobby horse ride through World War I has at times been tiresome and rough on my stiff fingers, weak eyes and nerves, but all in all it has been a great trip. These snatched mental visits into the past and mingling again with old friends, yet never getting more than a few yards from my rocking chair – I tell you this thing beats being dragged around sightseeing in a traveling tour. My writing hobby is like trying to ride a balking, bucking bronco and any cowboy will tell you that's no kindergarten stuff. If you know your stuff as a writer, you know that I was the victim of bucking and balks lots of times and the evidence is here in writing to show for itself, the bruises from the many falls I had. This tale is my answer to a Double Dog Dare to write my own story. If you are still inclined to judge me as being just another lazybones, I here issue you a Double Dog Dare to write your own story.

About the Author

Levi Early Hemrick was born July 20, 1890, in Clarke County, Georgia. His formal education was divided into two parts by World War I, which he regarded as his most formative education.

In 1914 he graduated from the Young Harris Junior College and, in 1917 when the United States entered the war, he was principal of a three-teacher rural school in DeKalb County, Georgia. He enlisted at once and fought with the U.S. Marines in Northern France, taking part in historic and decisive battles. He received a permanently disabling wound only five weeks before Armistice Day.

After the war, Hemrick majored in agriculture and earned his bachelor's and master's degrees from Peabody College for Teachers. He taught agriculture for ten years and was associated with the Farm Security Administration, but his persisting disability finally compelled him to abandon teaching, after which he was self-employed for the rest of his working life. He lived in retirement in Athens, Georgia, and was a member of the First United Methodist Church and American Legion Post 20.

He died on October 21, 1976, at the age of 86, following several months of failing health. With members of American Legion Post 20 serving as pallbearers, Hemrick was buried in Oconee Hill Cemetery in Athens, Georgia. His widow, Elizabeth Hemrick (born February 28, 1898) died on March 14, 1988.

CPSIA information can be obtained
at www.ICGtesting.com
Printed in the USA
FSOW01n1147281116
27901FS

9 780988 714588